Head to Toe Knits

Head to Toe Knits

25 colourful accessories for your home and children

Zoë Mellor

COLLINS & BROWN

For Tim, with love. Thanks for all your kind help and support – and cups of tea!

First published in Great Britain in 1998 by Collins & Brown Limited London House, Great Eastern Wharf, Parkgate Road, London SW11 4NQ

1 3 5 7 9 8 6 4 2

British Library Cataloguing-in-Publication Data:
A catalogue record for this book is available from the British Library.

ISBN 1-85585-616-6 (paperback edition)
ISBN 1-85585-660-3 (hardback edition)

Conceived, edited and designed by Collins & Brown Limited

Editor: Cath Senker
Designer: Jerry Goldie
Photography: Joey Toller

Reproduction by Hong Kong Graphic & Printing Ltd
Printed and bound in Spain by Graficromo S.A.

Contents

Introduction

Since I started my knitwear business, I have designed accessories to go with my clothing ideas and have found that people were keen to knit them. So, in this book there are lots of different designs and I hope you will be encouraged to try out a few. As most projects are small, even busy mums and children can have a go. I have included traditional ideas such as the Reindeer Scarf and Hat as well as more playful designs such as the Cat Hat.

I have recently moved house and this has inspired me to design accessories for the home, too, and I had great fun designing the bedspread, throw and different cushions. I know many adults love the idea of knitted cushions and bags – and they are surprisingly easy to make. I hope you have as much pleasure knitting up the designs as I did creating them. Happy Knitting!

Zoë Mellor

Cat hat
(see page 40)

Dotty duffel bag
(see page 41)

Heart cushion

(see page 42)

star hat and mittens
(see page 44)

stripy socks   **13**

(see page 45)

Tiger cushion
(see page 46)

Harlequin hat
(see page 48)

Patchwork scarf
(see page 49)

Denim satchel

(see page 51)

Boy and girl pencil case   **19**

(see page 52)

sherlock Holmes hat and mittens
(see page 53)

Playroom patched bedspread

(see page 55)

Daisy cushion
(see page 58)

Polar bear toy

(see page 59)

stripy bootees
(see page 60)

Diagonal denim throw and cushion

(see page 61)

knot hat
(see page 64)

Hearts and stars baby blanket
(see page 66)

Hearts and stars cushion

(see page 67)

Bunny shopping bag

(see page 68)

Rooster shoe bag 33
(see page 69)

Wee Willy Winkie hat
(see page 71)

stripy cushion
(see page 72)

star rucksack 37

(see page 73)

38 Tractor rucksack

(see page 76)

Reindeer scarf and and hat

(see page 77)

Cat hat

SIZES
to fit age 1-2 years (2-4 years, 5-6 years)

MATERIALS
Rowan Lightweight DK Wool 25g Skeins (used double throughout)

2 (2:3) skeins of main (M)

1 skein of contrast (A), and a small amount of B for ear stripes

1 pair 4½mm (US 7) needles and 1 pair 3¾mm (US 5) needles

TENSION
20sts to 28rows = 10cms (4ins) square using 4½mm (US 7) needles over stocking stitch.

ABBREVIATIONS
See page 79

METHOD
Using 3¾mm (US 5) needles and A doubled, cast on 123(131:139)sts, and work as folls:-

Change to M.

Row 1: *k1, p1* to last st, k1

Row 2: rib 23(25:27), *s1, k2tog, psso, p1, s1, k2tog, psso* rib 63(67:71), * * again, rib 23(25:27)

Row 3: rib 21(23:25), *p3tog, k1, p3tog* rib 59(63:67), * * again, rib 21(23:25)

Row 4: rib

Row 5: rib 19(21:23), *p3tog, k1, p3tog* rib 55(59:63), * * again, rib 19(21:23)

Row 6: rib 17(19:21), *s1, k2tog, psso, p1, s1, k2tog, psso, rib 51(55:59), * *again, rib 17(19:21)

(91:99:107sts)

Row 7: rib 20(22:24), yb, s1, yf, turn: *s1, rib 3, yb, s1, yf, turn: s1, rib 5, yb, s1, yf, turn, s1, rib 7, yb, s1, yf, turn: s1, rib 10, yb, s1, yf, turn, s1, rib 13, yb, s1, yf, turn: s1, rib 16, yb, s1, yf, turn, s1, rib 19, yb, s1, yf, turn: s1, rib 23, yb, s1, yf, turn, s1, rib 27, yb, s1, yf, turn:

SIZES 2 and 3: s1, rib 31, yb, s1, yf, turn, s1, rib 35, yb, s1, yf, turn:*

ALL SIZES: s1, rib 69(77:81), yb, s1, yf, turn, work from * * again, then s1, rib to end.

Change to 4½mm (US 7) needles and work as folls:-

Next row: (wrong side) p8(11:13), *p2tog, p22(23:24)* 3 times, p2tog, p9(11:14)   (87:95:103sts)

Work 16(16:18) rows stocking stitch. Start shaping for head. Foll correct size instructions. DECREASE ROWS GIVEN ONLY.

SIZE 1
Row 17: *k4, k2tog, k5* 7 times, k4, k2tog, k4

Row 20: *p4, p2tog, p4* 7 times, p4, p2tog, p3

Row 23: *k2, k2tog, k2, s1, k2tog, psso* 7 times, *k2, k2tog* twice

Row 25: *k1, k2tog, k3* 8 times

Row 26: p2tog, p1, *p2tog, p3* 7 times, p2tog

Row 27: k1, *k2tog, k1* 10 times

Row 28: p1, *p2tog* 10 times

SIZE 2
Row 17: *k5, k2tog, k5* 7 times, k5, k2tog, k4

Row 20: *p4, p2tog, p5* 7 times, p4, p2tog, p4

Row 23: *k3, k2tog, k5* 7 times, k3, k2tog, k4

Row 27: *k2, k2tog, k2, s1, k2tog, psso* 7 times, *k2, k2tog* twice

Row 29: *k1, k2tog, k3* 8 times

Row 31: *k2tog, k3* 8 times

Row 32: p2tog, p1, *p2tog, p2* 6 times, p2tog, p3

Row 33: k2tog, *k2tog, k1* 6 times, k2tog twice

Row 34: p1, *p2tog* 7 times

SIZE 3
Row 19: *k5, k2tog, k6* 7 times, k5, k2tog, k5

Row 22: *p5, p2tog, p5* 7 times, p5, p2tog, p4

Row 25: *k3, k2tog, k6* 7 times, k3, k2tog, k5

Row 28: *p2tog, p3* 15 times, p2tog, p2

Row 31: k1, *k2tog, k6* 7 times, k2tog, k4

Row 33: *k2tog, k5* 7 times, k2tog, k4

Row 35: k2, *k2tog, k1* 15 times

Row 37: k1, *k2tog* 15 times, k1

Row 38: p1, *p2tog* 8 times

ALL SIZES: run thread through rem sts and pull together. Fasten securely and sew back seam.

EARS
Using 4½mm (US 7) needles and A cast on 12sts.

Work in stocking stitch.

Rows 1-2: A

Rows 3-4: B

Rows 5-6: M

Rows 7-8: A

Row 9: Using B, k2, s1, k1, psso, k4, k2tog, k2

Row 10: B

Row 11: Using M, k2, s1, k1, psso, k2, k2tog, k2

Row 12: M

Row 13: Using A, k2, s1, k1, psso, k2tog, k2

Row 14: A

Row 15: Using B, s1, k1, psso, k2, k2tog
Row 16: Using B, p2tog, p2togb
Row 17: Using B, k2tog. Fasten off. Make second ear to match, then 2 more ears using M only.

MAKING UP
Place one plain ear and one striped ear right sides together and sew round edges leaving bottom edge open. Repeat for other ear.
Place ears in cat-like position on hat and fix securely. See photograph on pages 8-9.

Dotty duffel bag

SIZE
36cms (14ins) long by 23cms (9ins) diameter

MATERIALS
Rowan Handknit DK Cotton 50g Balls
6 balls Summer pudding 243 (M)
1 ball of foll colours:- Sailor blue 232 (A), Gooseberry 219 (B), Raspberry 240, Powder 217 and Sunkissed 231
1 pair 4mm (US 6) needles and a stitch holder

TENSION
20sts to 28rows = 10 cms (4ins) squared over stocking stitch, using 4mm (US 6) needles.

ABBREVIATIONS
See page 79

METHOD
POCKET
Using 4mm (US 6) needles and M, cast on 20sts and work 28 rows in stocking stitch. Leave on holder.

MAIN PART
Using 4mm (US 6) needles and M cast on 128sts and work as folls:-
Row 1: Using intarsia method for colour knitting, *k4A, k4B* to end
Row 2: *p4B, p4A* to end
Rows 3-6: as rows 1-2 twice
Change to M and work 72 rows in stocking stitch, placing motifs randomly and with your choice of contrast colours.
Row 73: Place pocket: patt 54, place next 20sts on holder, k across 20sts of pocket, patt 54
Cont to end of row 100
Rows 101-106: as rows 1-6

Row 107: Change to M, knit
Row 108: purl
Row 109: k2, *yrn, k2tog* to end
Row 110: purl
Row 111: Make hem: knit together 1st from needle and 1st from M loop from row 107, all across row
Row 112: purl
Row 113-116: Stocking stitch
Cast off. Weave in any loose ends.

POCKET TOP
Using 4mm (US 6) needles and M work 6 rows of k2, p2 rib. Cast off. Slipstitch pocket and pocket top into place.

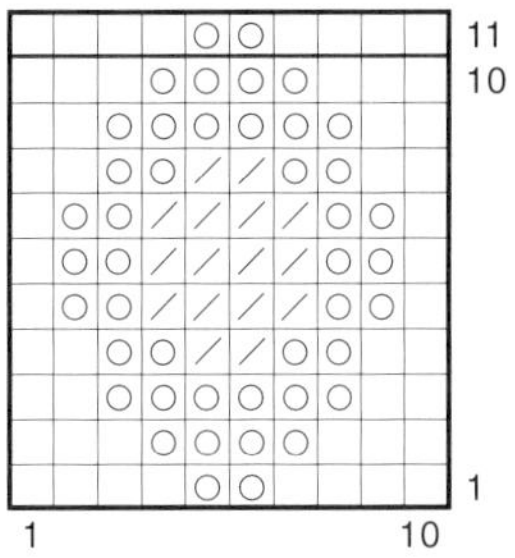

Chart grid with markings, row numbers 1, 10, 11 on right, 1 and 10 along bottom.

○ Contrast A
╱ Contrast B
☐ Main

BASE
Using 4mm (US 6) needles and M and with right side facing, pick up 128sts from cast-on edge. Work as folls:-
Row 1: purl
Rows 2-3: stocking stitch
Row 4: *k7, k2tog, k7* to end
Row 5 and alt rows: purl
Row 6: *k6, k2tog, k7* to end
Row 8: *k5, k2tog, k7* to end
Row 10: *k4, k2tog, k7* to end
Row 12: *k3, k2tog, k7* to end
Row 14: *k2, k2tog, k7* to end
Row 16: *k1, k2tog, k7* to end
Row 18: *k2tog, k7* to end
Row 20: k7, *k2tog, k6* to last 9sts, k2tog, k7
Row 22: k6, *k2tog, k5* to last 2sts, k2tog
Row 24: k5, *k2tog, k4* to last 2sts, k2tog
Row 26: k4, *k2tog, k3* to last 2sts, k2tog

Row 28: k3, *k2tog, k2* to last 2sts, k2tog

Row 30: k2, *k2tog, k1* to last 2sts, k2tog

Row 32: k1, *k2tog* to end

Row 34: *k2tog* to last st, k1

Thread yarn through sts and fasten securely. Join seam to complete circle.

INNER BASE

Using 4mm (US 6) needles and M cast on 128sts. Work rows 2-34 of base and fasten off as before.

STRAP

Using 4mm (US 6) needles and A cast on 5sts and work in stocking stitch until strap measures 122cms (48ins). Cast off. Allow edges to curl.

MAKING UP

With right sides together, join duffel bag side seam from base to top leaving 4 rows open at top in A/B

edging for strap. Turn down hem at top to inside, leaving picot as edging. Slip stitch into position. Cut a 23cm (9in) diameter circle out of heavy cardboard (use plate or bowl as guide). Place on bottom of bag and cover with inner base. Stitch into place.

Turn bag right side out. Thread strap through top hem. Cross over and sew to duffel bag at base of seam at back of bag.

Heart cushion

SIZE
36cms (14 ins) squared

MATERIALS
Rowan Handknit DK Cotton 50g Balls

3 balls Rosso 215 (M)

1 ball each of Turkish plum 277, Gooseberry 219, Basil 221, Powder 217, Flame 254, Popcorn 229 and Summer pudding 243

1 pair 4mm (US 6) needles and 1 pair 3¼mm (US 3) needles

4 buttons of your choice

1 36cm (14 in) square feather cushion pad

TENSION
20sts to 28rows = 10cms (4ins) squared over stocking stitch, using 4mm (US 6) needles.

ABBREVIATIONS
See page 79

DIAGRAM
See page 67

METHOD
Front: Using 4mm (US 6) needles cast on 70sts using appropriate colours and work in stocking stitch from chart. Use the intarsia method for all colour work. Cast off.

Back: Using 4mm (US 6) needles and M cast on 70sts and work 50 rows in stocking stitch. Change to 3¼mm (US 3) needles and work 2 rows k2, p2 rib.

Row 3: Rib 10, cast off 1st, *rib 15, cast off 1st* 3 times, rib 11

Row 4: Rib 11, yrn, *rib 15, yrn* 3 times, rib 10

Work 2 more rows in rib and cast off in contrast colour of your choice. Make second piece to match, omitting buttonholes.

POINTED EDGING
Using 4mm (US 6) needles and all colours randomly, but in complete pattern repeats, cast on 2sts.

Row 1: k2

Row 2: inc, k1

Row 3: k1, p1, inc

Row 4: inc, k1, p1, k1

Rows 5-8: moss stitch, inc at shaped edge on every row   (9sts)

Row 9: moss stitch

Rows 10-16: dec at shaped edge on each row, moss stitch   (2sts)

Repeat rows 1-16 until straight edge fits around edge of cushion.

MAKING UP
Pin edging around edge of front cushion. Place right sides together making sure the buttonhole back piece is under the button piece. The back of the cushion, once both back pieces are in place, will overlap to make a 36cm (14in) square to match the front.

Stitch around all four sides of cushion inside out, making sure you trap edging between the front and back pieces. Turn right side out and sew on buttons of your choice. Insert cushion pad.

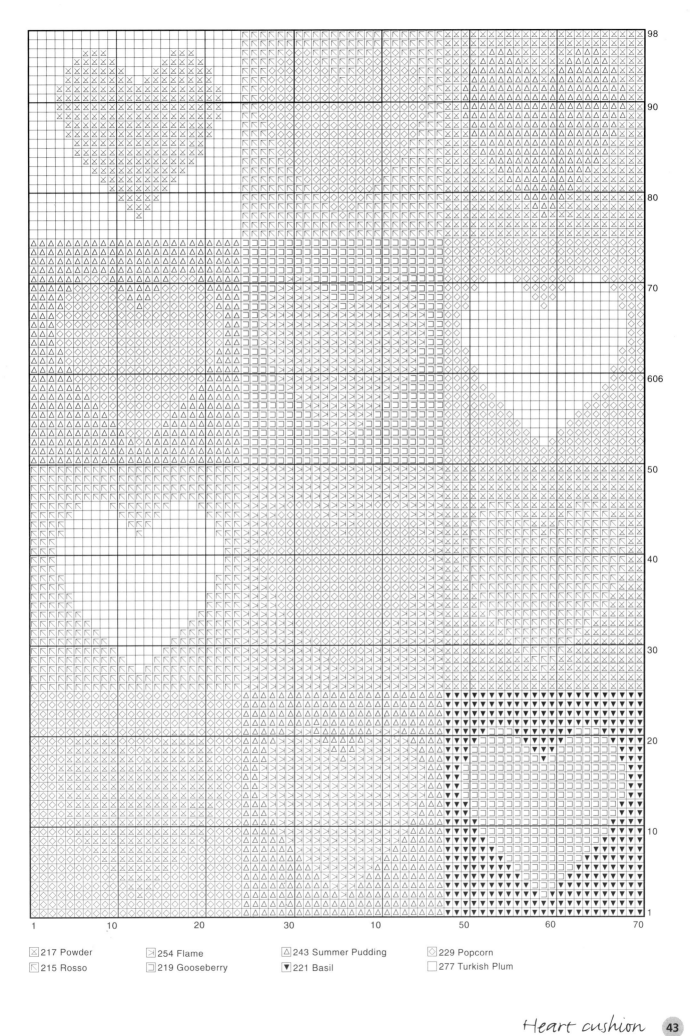

| ⊠ | 217 Powder | ↘ | 254 Flame | △ | 243 Summer Pudding | ◇ | 229 Popcorn |
| ↖ | 215 Rosso | ⊐ | 219 Gooseberry | ▼ | 221 Basil | ☐ | 277 Turkish Plum |

Heart cushion **43**

(see page 11)

star hat & mittens

Hat

SIZES
to fit age 1-2 years (2-4 years, 5-6 years)

MATERIALS
Rowan Lightweight DK Wool 25g Skeins

2(2:3) skeins Red 44 (M)

1 skein Navy 108 (C)

1 skein Yellow 13

1 pair 3¼mm (US 3) needles and 1 pair 3¾mm (US 5) needles

2 wooden beads (optional)

TENSION
24sts to 32rows = 10cms (4ins) square using 3¾mm (US 5) needles over stocking stitch.

ABBREVIATIONS
See page 79

METHOD
Using 3¼mm (US 3) needles and yellow cast on 91(101:109)sts Change to C and work 10(12:14) rows in k1, p1 rib.
Change to 3¾mm (US 5) needles, M and stocking stitch. Work 6(8:10) rows.
Next row: place star, k41(46:50)M, 1 yellow, 7M, 1 yellow, 41(46:50)M Complete motif using intarsia method of colour knitting.
Cont in M until work measures 14(15:16)cms, 5½(6:6½)ins.
Next row: cast off 20(22:24)sts, k5, cast off 40(46:50)sts, k5, cast off 20(22:24)sts

TIES (make 2)
With right side facing, using 3¾mm (US 5) needles and C, and working in stocking stitch, knit across 5sts. Continue until tie measures 20(23:25)cms, 8(9:10)ins. Cast off. Work other tie to match.

MAKING UP
Weave in any loose ends. Using chain stitch, outline star motif in C, if desired. Join centre back seam. Turn hat inside out and join top seam, using ties as corners and making sure that ties are not caught in seam. Turn right side out. Thread wooden bead (if desired) to tie and make a knot at end to secure. Tie both ties to fit child's head.

Mittens

SIZES
to fit age 1-2 years (2-4 years, 5-6 years)

MATERIALS
Rowan Lightweight DK Wool 25g Skeins

1 skein Red 44 (M)

1 skein Navy 108 (C)

1 skein Yellow 13

1 pair 3¼mm (US 3) needles

TENSION
26sts to 36rows = 10cms (4ins) square using 3¼mm (US 3) needles over stocking stitch.

ABBREVIATIONS
See page 79

RIGHT HAND
Using 3¼mm (US 3) needles and yellow cast on 33(38:43)sts. Change to C and work 10(12:14) rows in k1, p1 rib.
Change to stocking stitch and M, work 0(2:4) rows. ±

Shape for thumb
Row 1: k17(19:21), m1, k1(2:3), m1, k15(17:19)
Row 2 and alt rows: purl
Row 3: k17(19:21), m1, k3(4:5), m1, k15(17:19)
Row 5: start motif; k4(5:6)M, 1 yellow, 7M, 1 yellow, 4(5:6)M, m1, k5(6:7), m1, k15(17:19)
Cont with star motif and inc as set on alt rows to 43(48:53)sts, ending with purl row.
Next row: patt 28(31:34) turn; cast on 1st, p12(13:14) turn; cast on 1st, k13(14:15)
§On these 13(14:15)sts, work 5(7:9) rows.
Next row: k2tog twice, *s1, k2tog, psso* 1(2:3) times, k2tog 3(2:1) times. Break yarn and thread through sts, pulling tightly, and secure. Sew thumb seam.
With right side facing, rejoin yarn to base of thumb; pick up 3sts from base

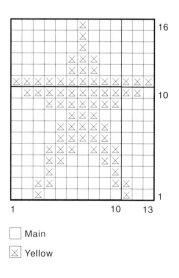

Chart

(chart 1 to 13 wide, 1 to 16 high, star motif)

□ Main

☒ Yellow

of thumb and complete row.

Complete star motif
Work further 6(8:10) rows in stocking stitch, using M.

Shape top
Row 1: k1, *s1, k1, psso, k12(14:16), k2tog, k1* twice
Rows 2-4: stocking stitch
Row 5: change to C, k1, *s1, k1, psso, k10(12:14), k2tog, k1* twice
Row 6: purl
Row 7: k1, *s1, k1, psso, k8(10:12), k2tog, k1* twice
Row 8: SIZE 1: purl
SIZES 2 and 3: p1, *p2tog, p8(10),

p2tog, p1* twice
Row 9: k1, *s1, k1, psso, k6(6:8), k2tog, k1* twice
Row 10: p1, *p2tog, p4(4:6). p2tog, p1* twice
Row 11: Cast off. §

LEFT HAND
Work as for right-hand mitten to ±

Shape for thumb
Row 1: k15(17:19), m1, k1(2:3), m1, k17(19:21)
Row 2 and alt rows: purl
Row 3: k15(17:19), m1, k3(4:5), m1, k17(19:21)

Row 5: start motif; k15(17:19), m1, k5(6:7), m1, k4(5:6)M, 1 yellow, 7M, 1 yellow, 4(5:6)M
Cont with star motif and inc as set on alt rows to 43(48:53)sts ending with a purl row.
Next row: patt 26(29:32), turn; cast on 1st, p12(13:14), turn; cast on 1st, k13(14:15)
Work § to § as on right-hand mitten.

MAKING UP
Weave in any loose ends. Outline stars in chain stitch using C, if desired. Join top and side seams.

stripy socks

SIZES
to fit age 1-2 years (3-4 years, 5-6 years)

MATERIALS
Rowan Lightweight DK Wool 25g Skeins
1 skein of foll colours (or 7 colours of your choice):- Navy 108 (M), Red 44, Purple 93, Sky blue 50, Green 90, Yellow 13 and Orange 25. We chose Navy as main.
Four 3mm (US 3) double-ended needles

TENSION
28sts to 40rows = 10cms (4ins) square using 3mm (US 3) over stocking stitch.

ABBREVIATIONS
See page 79

METHOD
Using M, cast on 42(48:54)sts, 14(16:18)sts on three 3mm (US 3) double-ended needles and using the fourth to knit with.
Work in rounds of k1, p1, rib and using colours randomly, continue until work measures 6(7:7)cms, 2½(3:3)ins. Divide sts for heel and instep.
Next round: using main colour: k10(11:12)sts, now slip the last k10(11:12)sts of the round onto the

other end of the same needle, giving 20(22:24)sts on needle which are used for the heel. Divide remaining sts onto 2 needles and leave for instep.
NOTE: Heel is worked on 2 needles in rows, not rounds, and in stocking stitch.
Row 1: sp, purl to end
Row 2: sk, knit to end
Repeat last 2 rows 4(5:6) times then row 1 again   (11:13:15 rows in total)
Next row: k13(14:15) sl, k1, psso, turn
Row 2: p7, p2tog, turn
Row 3: k7, s1, k1, psso, turn
Repeat last 2 rows 4(5:6) times, then row 2 again.
To complete heel

Next row: k4 (4sts remain on LH needle). Slip instep sts onto 1 needle. With spare needle knit the 4 remaining sts, knit up 6(7:8)sts along side of heel. Using 2nd needle, rib across instep sts. Using 3rd needle, pick up 6(7:8)sts along side of heel, k4 from needle.   42(48:54)sts
Rearrange sts to original 14(16:18) per needle, leaving centre of heel as beginning of round.
Work in rounds of 10(11:12)sts in stocking stitch, 22(26:30)sts in k1, p1 rib and 10(11:12)sts in stocking stitch, changing colours randomly, until foot

measures 9(12:15)cms, 3½(4¾:6)ins. Adjust length here to 3cms (1¼ ins) less than desired foot length.

Shape toe
Round 1: Using M: knit
Round 2: k7(9:10), k2tog, k2, s1, k1, psso, k15(18:21), k2tog, k2, s1, k1, psso, k8(9:11)
Round 3 and 5: knit
Round 4: k6(8:9), k2tog, k2, s1, k1, psso, k13(16:19), k2tog, k2, s1, k1, psso, k7(8:10)
Round 6: k5(7:8), k2tog, k2, s1, k1, psso, k11(14:17), k2tog, k2, s1, k1, psso, k6(7:9)
Round 7: k4(6:7), k2tog, k2, s1, k1, psso, k9(12:15), k2tog, k2, s1, k1, psso, k5(6:8)
Round 8: k3(5:6), k2tog, k2, s1, k1, psso, k7(10:13), k2tog, k2, s1, k1, psso, k4(5:7)
Round 9: k2(4:5), k2tog, k2, s1, k1, psso, k5(8:11), k2tog, k2, s1, k1, psso, k3(4:6)
Round 10: k1(3:4), k2tog, k2, s1, k1, psso, k3(6:9), k2tog, k2, s1, k1, psso, k2(3:5)
Round 11: Cast off.
Make second sock to match.

MAKING UP
Flat seam across toe. Weave in any loose ends.

Tiger cushion

SIZE
36cms (14 ins) squared

MATERIALS
Rowan Cotton Glace 50g Balls: 5 balls Oyster 730
Rowan Fine Cotton Chenille 50g Balls: 2 balls Black 413
1 pair 3¼mm (US 3) needles
3 buttons of your choice
36cm (14in) square cushion pad

TENSION
23sts to 32rows = 10cm (4in) square over stocking stitch using 3¼mm (US 3) needles.

ABBREVIATIONS
See page 79
DIAGRAM
See page 67

METHOD
Front: Using 3¼mm (US 3) needles and cotton glace cast on 85sts. Work from graph using stocking stitch and the intarsia method for colour knitting.

Back: Using 3¼mm (US 3) needles and cotton glace cast on 85sts and work 56 rows in stocking stitch. Change to k1, p1 rib and work 4 rows.
Row 5: *rib 19, cast off 3sts* 3 times, rib 19
Row 6: *rib 19, cast on 3sts* 3 times, rib 19
Rows 7-10: rib
Row 11: Cast off in rib.
Make second piece to match, omitting buttonholes.

MAKING UP
Weave in any loose ends. Place right sides together. Overlap back pieces, making sure that buttonhole piece is underneath button piece. Sew around the four sides. Turn rightside out and sew on buttons. Insert cushion pad.

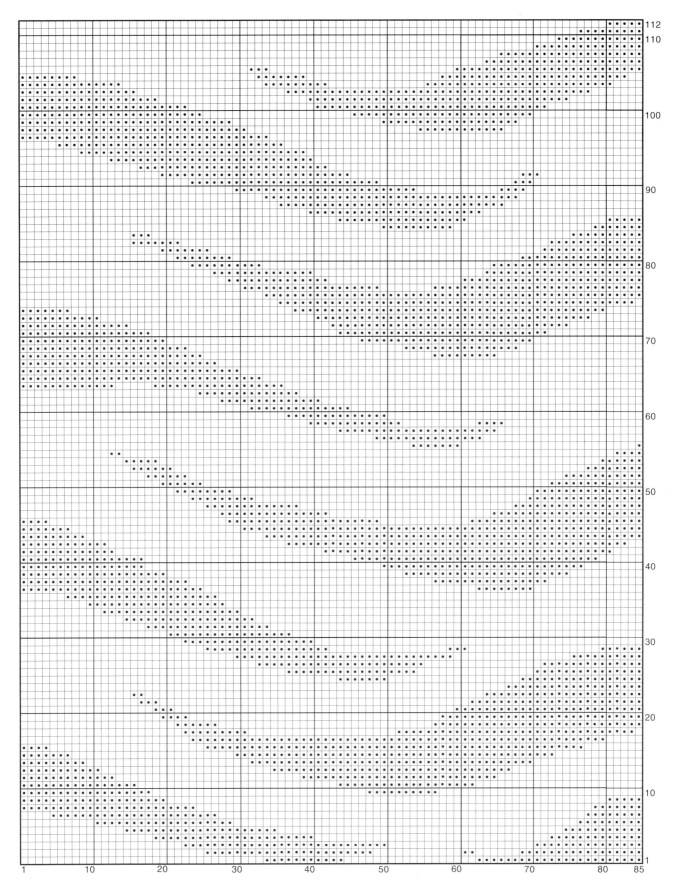

• 413 Fine Black Chenille   □ 730 Oyster

Tiger cushion   **47**

(see pages 14-15)

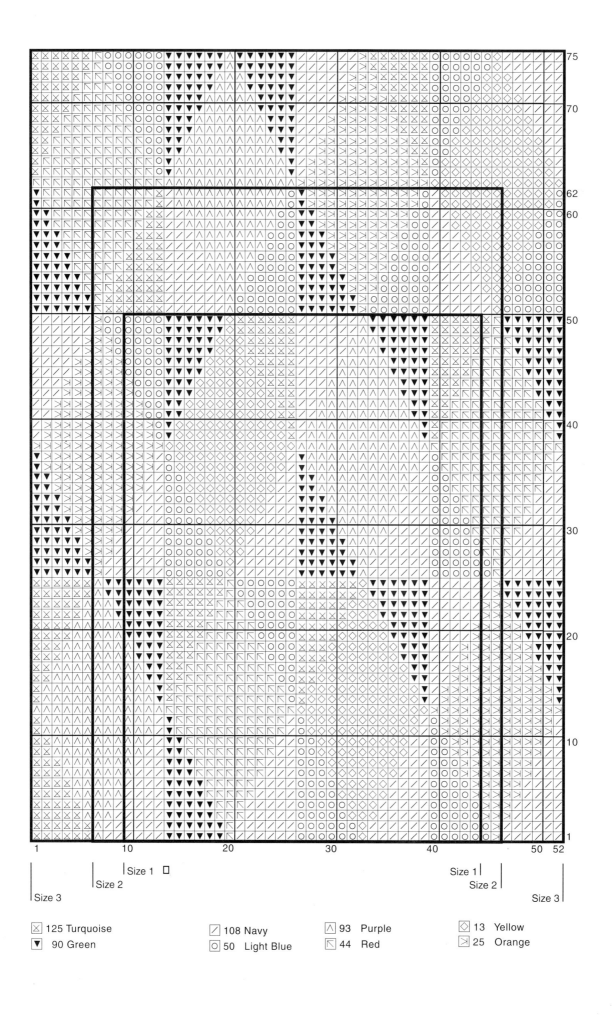

| ☒ | 125 | Turquoise | ◹ | 108 | Navy | ⋀ | 93 | Purple | ◇ | 13 | Yellow |
| ▼ | 90 | Green | ◯ | 50 | Light Blue | ⬉ | 44 | Red | ⊳ | 25 | Orange |

Harlequin hat
(see page 16)

Harlequin hat

SIZES
To fit age 0-1 years (age 2-4 years, 5-6 years)

MATERIALS
Rowan Lightweight DK Wool 25g Skeins (used doubled throughout this design)
3 skeins Red 44 (M)
1 skein of each of the foll colours:- Turquoise 125, Green 90, Navy 108, Sky blue 50, Purple 93, Yellow 13 and Orange 25
1 pair 4½mm (US 7) needles and 1 pair 3¾mm (US 5) needles

TENSION
20sts to 28rows = 10cms (4ins) squared over stocking stitch, using 4½mm (US 7) needles.

ABBREVIATIONS
See page 79

METHOD
Using 3¾mm (US 5) needles and Red doubled cast on 35 (40:52)sts and knit 8 rows of k1, p1 rib.

Change to 4½mm (US 7) needles and stocking stitch. Follow the graph for the required size, still using yarns doubled and using the intarsia method for colour knitting.
Change back to 3¾mm (US 5) needles and Red doubled.
SIZES 1 AND 2: knit 1 row
SIZE 3 ONLY: purl 1 row
Then ALL SIZES: Work 8 rows in k1, p1 rib and cast off in rib.

MAKING UP
Sew up side seams. Weave in any loose ends. Make 2 pom-poms and attach them to the corners of the hat to add weight, so corners flop like a jester's hat.

Patchwork scarf

SIZE
21cms (8½ins) wide by 110cms (43ins) long. One size.

MATERIALS
Rowan Lightweight DK Wool 25g Skeins
1 skein of foll colours:- Navy 108, Red 44, Purple 93, Sky blue 50, Green 90, Yellow 13 and Orange 25
1 pair 3¾mm (US 5) needles

TENSION
24sts to 32rows = 10cms (4ins) square using 3¾mm (US 5) over stocking stitch.

ABBREVIATIONS
See page 79

METHOD
Using 3¾mm (US 5) needles cast on 17sts in navy (C), 17sts in red (B) and 17sts in yellow (A).   (51sts)
Work rows 1-24 from graph.
Row 25: knit 17sts sky blue (D), 17sts green (E), 17sts orange (F)
Rows 26-48: Foll graph.
This completes patt repeat. Cont as folls. NB: Rows 1 and 25 are always knit rows, after 1st patt repeat.

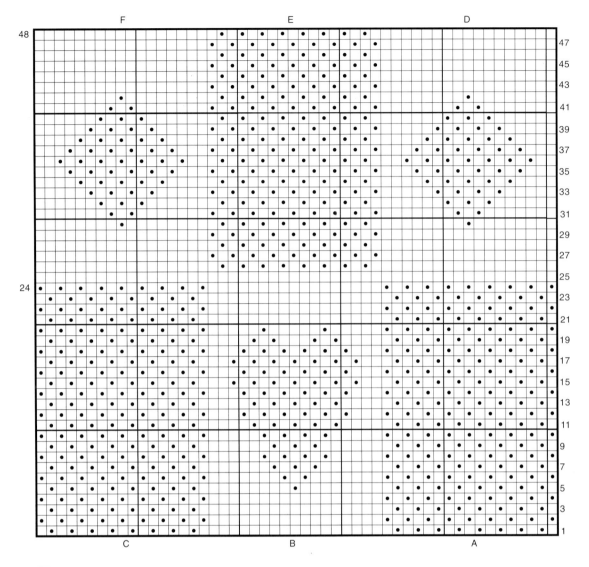

☐ Knit on rightside, Purl on wrongside

• Purl on rightside, Knit on wrongside

2nd patt repeat
A = navy, B = purple, C = red,
D = orange, E = yellow, F = green

3rd patt repeat
A = purple, B = sky blue, C = navy,
D = yellow, E = green, F = orange

4th patt repeat
A = sky blue, B = navy, C = red,
D = red, E = yellow, F = green

5th patt repeat
A = purple, B = orange, C = sky blue,
D = green, E = navy, F = red

6th patt repeat
A = sky blue, B = yellow, C = orange,
D = red, E = purple, F = navy

7th patt repeat
A = yellow, B = navy, C = red,
D = sky blue, E = orange, F = green

8th patt repeat
A = navy, B = red, C = purple
Row 25: cast off in appropriate
colours.

MAKING UP
Weave in any loose ends and
press using a damp cloth over
the work.

Denim satchel

SIZE
31cms (12ins) wide by 24cms (9½ins) high by 7cms (3ins) deep, when shrunk

MATERIALS
Rowan Denim 50g Balls
6 balls Nashville 225
1 pair 4mm (US 6) needles
2 buttons of your choice
½ metre (20in) of lining fabric of your choice

TENSION
20sts to 28rows = 10 cms (4ins) squared over stocking stitch, using 4mm (US 6) needles.

ABBREVIATIONS
See page 79

METHOD
Using 4mm (US 6) needles cast on 57sts and work as folls:-
Row 1: *k1, p1* to last st, k1
Row 2: *k1, p1* 23 times, yb, sp, yf, turn
Row 3: sp, *p1, k1* 17 times, p1, yb, sp, yf, turn
Row 4: sp, *p1, k1* 19 times, yf, sp, yb, turn
Row 5: sp, *k1, p1* 20 times, k1, yf, sp, yb, turn
Row 6: sp, *k1, p1* 22 times, yb, sp, yf, turn
Row 7: sp, *p1, k1* 23 times, p1, yb, sp, yf, turn
Row 8: sp, *p1, k1* 24 times, p1, yb, sp, yf, turn
Row 9: sp, *p1, k1* 5 times, cast off 3sts, *k1, p1* 12 times, k1, cast off 3sts, *k1, p1* 5 times, yb, sp, yf, turn
Row 10: sp, *p1, k1* 5 times, cast on 3sts, *k1, p1* 12 times, k1, cast on 3sts, *k1, p1* 6 times, k1
Row 11: *k1, p1* 28 times, k1
Cont in moss stitch until work measures 18.5cms (7½ins).
Cast on 15sts beg of next 2 rows.
Cont in moss stitch until work measures 47cms (18½ins).
Cast off 15sts beg next 2 rows.
Cont in moss stitch until work measures 56cms (22ins).

Next row: k1, *k5, inc in next st, k5*
5 times, k1 (62sts)
Next row: purl
Cont in stocking stitch until work measures 83cms (32½ins) ending with KNIT row.
Next row: p1, *p5, p2tog, p5*
5 times, p1 (57sts)
Work 6 rows in moss stitch. Cast off in moss stitch.

STRAP
Using 4mm (US 6) needles cast on 9sts and work in moss stitch until strap measures 115cms (45ins).
Cast off.

MAKING UP
Machine wash both parts in separate 60° C hot wash with soap powder and tumble dry to shrink. Rowan Denim will fade as jeans do with every wash but most colour will come out in this initial wash.
Lay shrunk pieces on a flat surface and trace outline of bag on to lining

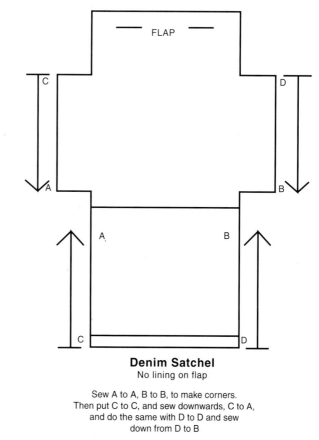

Denim Satchel
No lining on flap

Sew A to A, B to B, to make corners.
Then put C to C, and sew downwards, C to A,
and do the same with D to D and sew
down from D to B

fabric, omitting flap, so lining will go C to D, horizontally. Allow a 1cm (½in) seam allowance and cut out fabric lining. Look at diagram.
For knitting and lining, first sew up A to A, and B to B, making corners. Then sew side seams C to C and D to D and sew each side downwards C to A, D to B. You should now have the satchel shape. Then machine the lining so it is the same shape as the bag. Now fit lining into satchel shape. All seams should face each other. Pin the lining into place, turning under top edge of lining neatly. Using navy for the bobbin and a top thread to match lining, and hem around inside top edge of bag opening.

Now line strap in same fabric, again leaving a 1cm (½in) seam allowance all the way round strap. Pin lining to strap, tucking raw edges neatly to inside of strap as you pin. Machine lining into position.
Sew strap to sides of bag right side out. Sew on buttons to correspond with buttonholes on flap.

Boy and girl pencil case

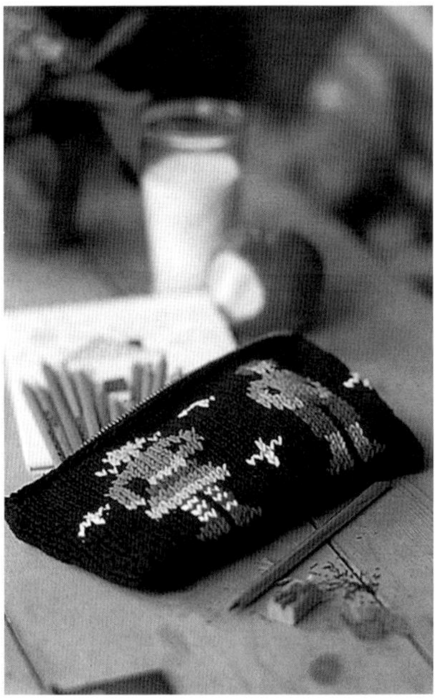

SIZE

23cms (9ins) wide by 13cms (5ins) deep

MATERIALS

Rowan Handknit DK Cotton 50g Balls
1 ball Turkish plum 277 (M)
Small amounts of Flame 254, Popcorn 229, Powder 217, Bleached 263, Rosso 215, Basil 221, Raspberry 240 and Port 245
1 pair 4mm (US 6) needles
1 navy blue zip measuring 23cms (9ins)

TENSION

20sts to 28rows = 10cms (4ins) squared over stocking stitch, using 4mm (US 6) needles.

ABBREVIATIONS

See page 79

METHOD AND MAKING UP

Using 4mm (US 6) needles and M cast on 48sts and work in stocking stitch from chart. Cast off. Do all colour work using the intarsia method of knitting.
Knit second piece to match. Stitch side seams and base. Pin zip into place and stitch.
Weave in any loose ends.

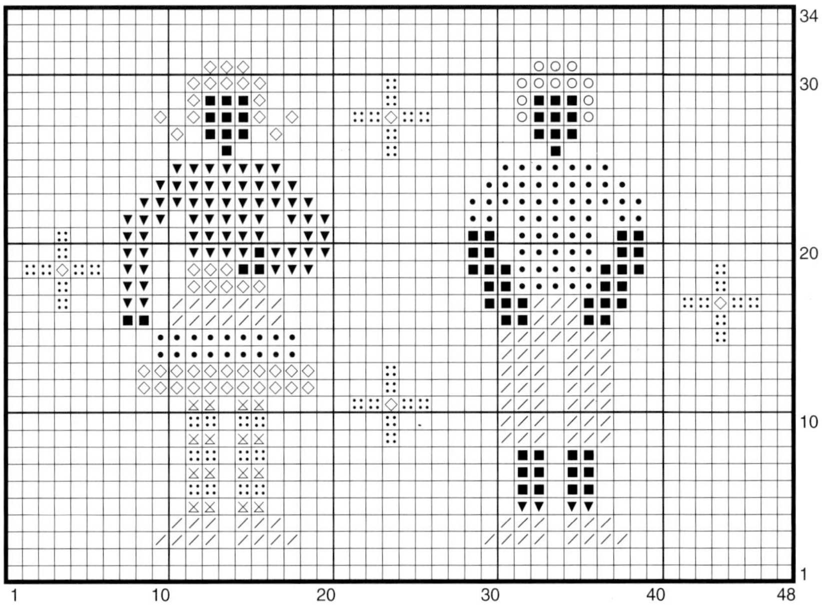

277 Turkish Plum (M)
221 Basil
240 Raspberry
254 Flame
229 Popcorn
245 Port
217 Powder
215 Rosso
263 Bleached

sherlock Holmes hat & mittens

Hat

SIZES
to fit age 1-2 years (2-4 years, 5-6 years)

MATERIALS
Rowan Lightweight DK Wool 25g Skeins (used double throughout)
2(3:3) skeins of main (M) of your choice
1(1:2) skeins contrast (C) of your choice
1 pair 4½mm (US 7) needles and 1 pair 3¾mm (US 5) needles
2 buttons of your choice

TENSION
20sts to 28rows = 10cms (4ins) square using 4½mm (US 7) needles over stocking stitch.

ABBREVIATIONS
See page 79

METHOD
PART A: EARFLAP
Using 3¾mm (US 5) needles and M cast on 9sts. Work in k1, p1 rib, foll correct size instructions.

SIZE 1
Row 1: *k1, p1* to last st, k1
Row 2: rib, inc each end
Row 3: rib
Rows 4-7: as rows 2-3 twice
Rows 8-9: rib
Row 10: as row 2   (17sts)
Rows 11-14: rib
Row 15: rib to end, cast on 14sts
Rows 16-26: rib, leave on spare needle

SIZE 2
Rows 1-7: as size 1
Row 8: rib, inc each end
Rows 9-11: rib
Row 12: as row 8   (19sts)
Rows 13-16: rib
Row 17: rib to end, cast on 15sts
Rows 18-28: rib, leave on spare needle

SIZE 3
Row 1: as size 1
Rows 2-3: rib, inc each end
Rows 4-6: as rows 1-3
Row 7: rib
Row 8: as row 2
Rows 9-19: as rows 7-8   (21sts)
Rows 11-16: rib
Row 17: rib to end, cast on 16sts
Rows 18-28: rib, leave on spare needle

PART B: TURN-UP FLAP
Using 3¾mm (US 5) needles and M cast on 25(27:29)sts. Work 10 rows in k1, p1 rib. Leave on spare needle.

PART C: 2ND EARFLAP
As part A until end of row 14(16:16)
Row 15 (17:17): rib
Row 16 (18:18): rib to end, cast on 14(15:16)sts
Rows 17-26 (18-28:18-28): rib
ALL SIZES
Next row: rib across part C, then part B, then part A making sure rib sequence is correct.   (87:95:103sts)
Work 5 more rows in rib.
Change to 4½mm (US 7) needles, stocking stitch and work in stripe patt of 2 rows C, 2 rows M.
Work 18(18:20) rows, then foll correct size instructions.

DECREASE ROWS GIVEN ONLY

SIZE 1
Row 19: *k4, k2tog, k5* 7 times, k4, k2tog, k4
Row 22: *p4, p2tog, p4* 7 times, p4, p2tog, p3
Row 25: *k2, k2tog, k2, s1, k2tog, psso* 7 times, *k2, k2tog* twice
Row 27: *k1, k2tog, k3* 8 times
Row 28: p2tog, p1, *p2tog, p3* 7 times, p2tog
Row 29: k1, *k2tog, k1* 10 times
Row 30: p1, *p2tog* 10 times

SIZE 2
Row 19: *k5, k2tog, k5* 7 times, k5, k2tog, k4
Row 22: *p4, p2tog, p5* 7 times, p4, p2tog, p4
Row 25: *k3, k2tog, k5* 7 times, k3, k2tog, k4
Row 29: *k2, k2tog, k2, s1, k2tog, psso* 7 times, *k2, k2tog* twice
Row 31: *k1, k2tog, k3* 8 times
Row 33: *k2tog, k3* 8 times
Row 34: p2tog, p1, *p2tog, p2* 6 times, p2tog, p3
Row 35: k2tog, *k2tog, k1* 6 times, k2tog twice
Row 36: p1, *p2tog* 7 times

SIZE 3
Row 21: *k5, k2tog, k6* 7 times, k5, k2tog, k5

Row 24: *p5, p2tog, p5* 7 times, p5, p2tog, p4

Row 27: *k3, k2tog, k6* 7 times, k3, k2tog, k5

Row 30: *p2tog, p3* 15 times, p2tog, p2

Row 33: k1, *k2tog, k6* 7 times, k2tog, k4

Row 35: *k2tog, k5* 7 times, k2tog, k4

Row 37: k2, *k2tog, k1* 15 times

Row 39: k1, *k2tog* 15 times, k1

Row 40: p1, *p2tog* 8 times

ALL SIZES

Run thread through rem sts and pull together. Fasten securely and sew back seam.

MAKING UP

Weave in any loose ends. Turn up front flap and secure with buttons (see photograph on pages 20-21). Cut three 60cm (24in) lengths of M. Thread half the length through bottom centre of earflap, and taking one end from front and one from back make plait with 2 ends per strand. Knot at end and trim. Do this on both earflaps.

Mittens

SIZES

to fit age 1-2 years (2-4 years, 5-6 years)

MATERIALS

Rowan Lightweight DK 25g Wool Skeins (used double throughout)

1(1:2) skeins of main (M) of your choice

1(1:1) skeins contrast (C) of your choice

1 pair 3¼mm (US 3) needles

TENSION

23sts to 30rows = 10cms (4ins) square using 3¼mm (US 3) needles over stocking stitch.

ABBREVIATIONS

See page 79

METHOD

RIGHT-HAND MITTEN

Cuff: *Using 3¼mm (US 3) needles and C, cast on 29(33:38)sts. Change to M and work 19(23:27) rows in k1, p1 rib.

Main part of mitten: Change to stocking stitch. Work in striped patt of 2 rows in each colour.

NOTE: SIZES 1 and 3 start 2 rows C

SIZE 2 starts 2 rows M

Work: 0(2:4) rows*

Start thumb shaping as folls:-

Row 1: k15(17:19), m1, k1(1:2), m1, k13(15:17)

Row 2: purl

Row 3: k15(17:19), m1, k3(3:4), m1, k13(15:17)

Row 4: purl

Row 5: k15(17:19), m1, k5(5:6), m1, k13(15:17)

Row 6: purl

Rows 7-10: Cont increases as set on alt rows to 39(43:48) sts.

Row 11: Work thumb, k26(28:31) turn, cast on 1st, p12(12:13) turn, cast on 1st, k13(13:14)

Work thumb as folls:-

§On these 13(13:14)sts work 5(7:9) rows in stocking stitch using M.

Next row: k2tog twice, *s1, k2tog, psso* 1(1:2) times, k2tog, 3(3:2) times. Break yarn, thread through sts and pull tight. Secure and sew thumb seam. With right side facing rejoin yarn to base of thumb. Pick up 3sts from base of thumb and complete row 11.

Work 7(9:11) more rows in striped patt.

Shape top as folls:-

Row 1: k1, *s1, k1, psso, k10(12:14), k2tog, k1* twice

Rows 2-4: stocking stitch

Row 5: k1, *s1, k1, psso, k8(10:12), k2tog, k1* twice

Row 6: purl

Row 7: k1, *s1, k1, psso, k6(8:10), k2tog, k1* twice

Row 8: SIZE 1: purl

SIZES 2 and 3: p1, *p2tog, p6(8), p2togb, p1, *twice

Row 9: k1, *s1, k1, psso, k4(4:6), k2tog, k1* twice

Row 10: p1, *p2tog, p2(2:4), p2togb, p1* twice

Row 11: Cast off. §

LEFT-HAND MITTEN

Cuff: Work * to * as on right-hand mitten.

Shape thumb as folls:-

Row 1: k13(15:17), m1, k1(1:2), m1, k15(17:19)

Row 2: purl

Row 3: k13(15:17), m1, k3(3:4), m1, k15(17:19)

Cont as set increasing 2sts on alt rows to end of row 10. (39:43:48sts)

Row 11: k24(26:29) turn; cast on 1st,
p12(12:13) turn; cast on 1st,
k13(13:14)
Then work from § to § as on right-
hand mitten.

MAKING UP
Join top and side seam, reversing
fabric for cuff seam. Weave in any
loose ends.

Playroom patched bedspread

SIZE
To fit child's single bed, 175cms (70ins) long by 132cms (52ins) wide

MATERIALS
Rowan Handknit DK Cotton 50g Balls

18 balls Royal 294 (M)

10 balls Powder 217

11 balls Summer pudding 243

10 balls Basil 221

8 balls Sunkissed 231

8 balls Popcorn 229

8 balls Gooseberry 219

6 balls Raspberry 240

1 pair 4mm (US 6) needles and 1 pair 3¼mm (US 3) needles

TENSION
20sts to 28rows = 10cms (4ins)
squared over stocking stitch, using
4mm (US 6) needles.

ABBREVIATIONS
See page 79

METHOD
Using 4mm (US 6) needles cast on
30sts and make 8 of each motif chart
using the intarsia method for picture
knitting in stocking stitch. Cast off.
Weave in any loose ends once
knitted.
Note: We knitted 4 heart squares
using Sunkissed 231 as the
background colour and 4 using
Popcorn 229 as the background
colour, totalling 8 squares. We also
knitted the flower chart 4 times using
Sunkissed 231 on the petal part and

then 4 times using Popcorn 229 on
the petal part, again knitting 8
squares in total.
You should now have 40 squares, 8
of each motif.
To make stripy squares knit 10 squares
of each stripe sequence as folls:-

First sequence
Using 4mm (US 6) needles cast on
30sts in Powder 217 and knit in
stocking stitch as folls:-
Rows 1-3: Powder 217
Rows 4-5: Raspberry 240
Rows 6-9: Summer pudding 243
Rows 10-12: Popcorn 229
Rows 13-14: Basil 221
Rows 15-17: Royal 294
Rows 18-21: Powder 217
Rows 22-24: Raspberry 240
Rows 25-28: Summer pudding 243
Rows 29-30: Basil 221

Rows 31-33: Royal 294
Rows 34-37: Gooseberry 219
Rows 38-40: Sunkissed 231
Rows 41-42: Popcorn 229
Cast off in last colour.

Second sequence
Using 4mm (US 6) needles cast on
30sts in Gooseberry 219 and knit in
stocking stitch as folls:-
Rows 1-3: Gooseberry 219
Rows 4-5: Popcorn 229
Rows 6-9: Powder 217
Rows 10-12: Summer pudding 243
Rows 13-14: Sunkissed 231
Rows 15-17: Royal 294
Rows 18-21: Powder 217
Rows 22-24: Basil 221
Rows 25-28: Sunkissed 231
Rows 29-30: Summer pudding 243
Rows 31-33: Popcorn 229
Rows 34-37: Royal 294
Rows 38-39: Gooseberry 219
Rows 40-42: Powder 217
Cast off in last colour.

Playroom patched bedspread

(see pages 22-23)

Third sequence

Using 4mm (US 6) needles cast on 30sts in Summer pudding 243 and knit in stocking stitch as folls:-

Rows 1-3: Summer pudding 243
Rows 4-5: Popcorn 229
Rows 6-7: Powder 217
Rows 8-9: Gooseberry 219
Rows 10-12: Summer pudding 243
Rows 13-14: Sunkissed 231
Rows 15-17: Popcorn 229
Rows 18-21: Summer pudding 243
Rows 22-24: Basil 221
Rows 25-26: Popcorn 229
Rows 27-28: Gooseberry 219
Rows 29-30: Summer pudding 243
Rows 31-33: Royal 294
Rows 34-37: Powder 217
Rows 38-40: Popcorn 229
Rows 41-42: Summer pudding 243
Cast off in last colour.

Fourth sequence

Using 4mm (US 6) needles cast on 30sts in Summer pudding 243 and knit in stocking stitch as folls:-

Rows 1-3: Summer pudding 243
Rows 4-5: Royal 294
Rows 6-9: Gooseberry 219
Rows 10-12: Summer pudding 243
Rows 13-14: Basil 221
Rows 15-17: Royal 294
Rows 18-21: Powder 217
Rows 22-24: Gooseberry 219
Rows 25-28: Royal 294
Rows 29-30: Raspberry 240
Rows 31-33: Summer pudding 243
Rows 34-37: Popcorn 229
Rows 38-40: Gooseberry 219
Rows 41-42: Basil 221
Cast off in last colour.

EDGING (make 4)

Using 3¼mm (US 3) needles and Royal 294, cast on 2sts and work as folls:-

Row 1: k1, p1
Row 2: inc, k1
Row 3: k1, p1, inc
Row 4: inc, k1, p1, k1
Rows 5-9: Cont as set, inc same edge and moss st   (11sts)
Cont in moss stitch until work, when slightly stretched, measures same as side of blanket, omitting mitred corner.

Make mitred corner at other end by decreasing on same side each row to 2 sts. Work 1 row. Cast off.

NOTE: Make sure mitre is worked so that there is a short side to sew to patch part of bedspread. Leave longer edge to form edge of bedspread.

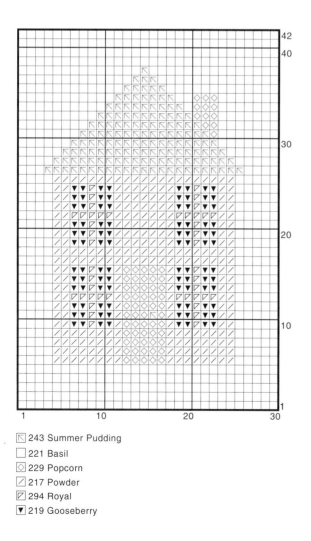

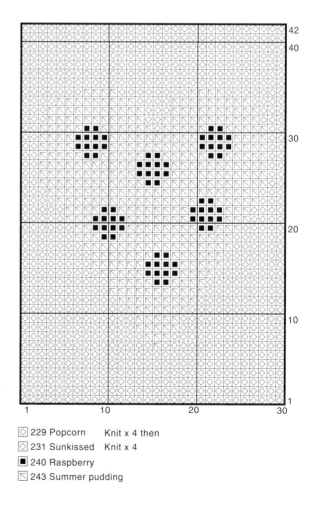

� 243 Summer Pudding
☐ 221 Basil
◇ 229 Popcorn
／ 217 Powder
▽ 294 Royal
▼ 219 Gooseberry

◇ 229 Popcorn   Knit x 4 then
◇ 231 Sunkissed   Knit x 4
■ 240 Raspberry
N 243 Summer pudding

Playroom patched bedspread
(see pages 22-23)

MAKING UP

Lay out all pieces on the floor and arrange 8 squares by 10 rows of squares to make bedspread shape. Alternate stripy and motif squares, making sure no two the same are next to each other. Once you are happy with your layout, number the squares so you remember the sequence, perhaps with a sticker on the back of each one. Stitch them together using a flat seam to avoid any bulky seams at back of work. Once you have sewn all the squares together stitch the moss st edging around all 4 sides and sew up mitred corners. Weave in any loose ends.

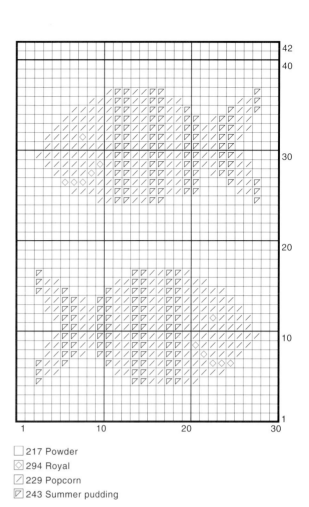

☐ 217 Powder
◇ 294 Royal
⁄ 229 Popcorn
▽ 243 Summer pudding

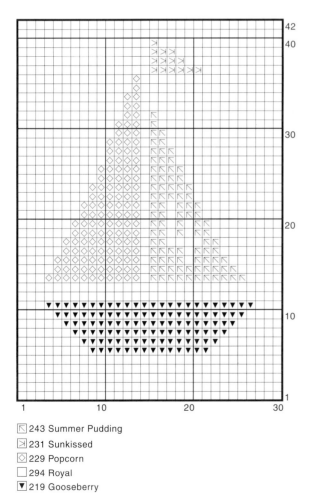

◣ 243 Summer Pudding
⊠ 231 Sunkissed
◇ 229 Popcorn
☐ 294 Royal
▼ 219 Gooseberry

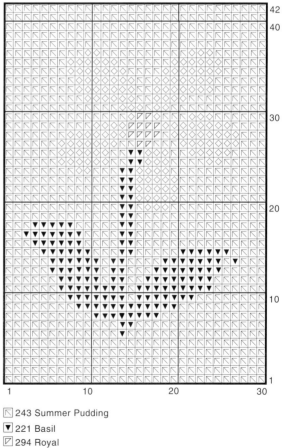

◣ 243 Summer Pudding
▼ 221 Basil
▽ 294 Royal
◇ 229 Popcorn   Knit x4 then
◇ 231 Sunkissed Knit x4

Playroom patched bedspread **57**

(see pages 22-23)

Daisy cushion

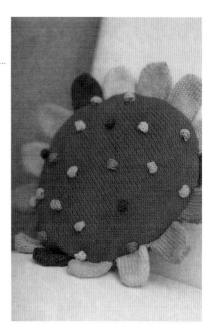

SIZE
31cms (12ins) diameter circle

MATERIALS
Rowan Handknit DK Cotton 50g Balls

3 balls Summer pudding 243 (M)

1 ball each of Gooseberry 219, Popcorn 229, Powder 217, Raspberry 240, Sunkissed 231 and Royal 294

1 pair 4mm (US 6) needles and 1 pair 3¼mm (US 3) needles

3 buttons of your choice

One 31cm (12in) diameter circular cushion pad

TENSION
20sts to 28rows = 10cms (4ins) squared over stocking stitch, using 4mm (US 6) needles.

ABBREVIATIONS
See page 79

METHOD
Front circle: Using Summer pudding 243 cast on 12sts. Work in stocking stitch as folls:-

Rows1-2: Cast on 4sts (at beg of each row).

Rows 3-6: Cast on 3sts

Rows 7-12: Cast on 2sts

Rows 13-20: Cast on 1st

Row 21: knit

Rows 22-25: Cast on 1st

Rows 26-27: stocking st

Rows 28-29: Cast on 1st

Rows 30-33: stocking st

Rows 34-35: Cast on 1st   (60sts)

Rows 36-49: stocking st

Rows 50-51: Cast off 1st

Rows 52-55: stocking st

Rows 56-57: Cast off 1st

Rows 58-59: stocking st

Rows 60-63: Cast off 1st

Row 64: purl

Rows 65-72: Cast off 1st

Rows 73-78: Cast off 2sts

Rows 79-82 : Cast off 3sts

Rows 83-84: Cast off 4sts

Row 85: Cast off.

Back circle: Knit as front to end of row 42.

Change to 3¼mm (US 3) needles and work in moss stitch for 4 rows.

Row 5: *moss 14, cast off 1st* 3 times, moss 15

Row 6: moss 15, *yrn, moss 14* 3 times

Rows 7-8: moss

Cast off.

Work another piece to match, omitting buttonholes.

BOBBLES (make 20)
Using a different colour of your choice for each bobble and 4mm (US 6) needles, cast on 2sts – leaving 5cm (2ins) of yarn for tying – and work as folls:-

Row 1: inc, inc

Row 2: purl

Row 3: knit

Row 4: purl

Row 5: k2tog twice

Row 6: p2tog, fasten off leaving 5cm (2ins) of yarn for tying.

Arrange bobbles on cushion front, take loose ends through the material to back of work making sure there is 1st between ends. Tie securely.

PETALS (make 20)
Using a different colour of your choice for each petal and 4mm (US 6) needles, cast on 12sts and work in stocking st as folls:-

Rows 1-12: stocking st

Row 13: k2tog, work to last 2sts, k2tog

Row 14: purl

Rows 15-18: as rows 13-14, twice

Row 19: knit

Row 20: inc, work to last st, inc

Rows 21-24: as rows 19-20, twice

Rows 25-36: stocking stitch

Row 37: Cast off.

MAKING UP
Fold each petal in half and stitch side seams. Arrange petals around front cushion and pin or tack into place with points towards cushion centre. Place back half circles over cushion front, right sides together, and overlapping, making sure buttonhole half circle is underneath plain half circle. Sew securely through all thicknesses trapping the petals in place as you sew. Turn right side out. Sew on buttons. Insert cushion pad.

Polar bear toy

SIZE
Size will vary depending on your tension and weight of yarn

MATERIALS
We used Rowan Designer DK Wool 50g Balls (but for a bigger bear you could use Rowan Magpie Aran)

1 ball White 649 (M)

Small amount of Black 062 for eyes and nose

1 bag of white toy stuffing or carded fleece

1 pair 4mm (US 6) needles and a darning needle to embroider face

METHOD
Using 4mm (US 6) needles and M cast on 40sts and knit 20 rows. Cast off 10sts at beginning of next 2 rows. Knit 18 rows, then cast on 10sts at beginning of next 2 rows. Knit 20 rows. Cast off 10sts at beginning of next 2 rows. Knit 2 rows, then knit 2tog at each end of alternate rows until 2sts remain. Cast off.

MAKING UP
See diagram.

Fold A to B and sew up leg. Repeat with C to D, E to F, and G to H, until you have 4 pockets for legs. Stuff all 4 with stuffing.

Fold L to L, and K to K, and sew up triangular face. Stuff to make face rounder.

Fill bear with stuffing and stitch closed under belly to M.

Next, pinch a small piece of knitting either side of the face and pull up the ears. Make ears by wrapping pinched up knitting with white yarn and securing ear shape with a stitch. To finish, embroider eyes, nose and mouth using black yarn. Tuck in any loose ends.

Polar Bear Diagram

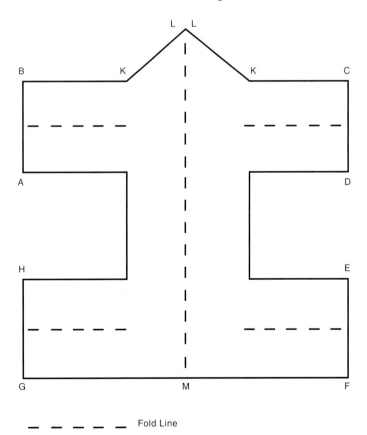

Fold Line

stripy bootees

SIZE
To fit baby 0-12 months

MATERIALS
Rowan Lightweight DK Wool 25g Skeins
2 skeins Navy 108 (M)
1 skein Red 44
1 skein Yellow 13
1 pair 3mm (US 3) needles

TENSION
32sts and 40 rows = 10cms (4ins)
square using 3mm (US 3) over
stocking stitch.

ABBREVIATIONS
See page 79

METHOD
Sole: Using 3mm (US 3) needles
and M, cast on 53sts.
Row 1: *inc, k24, inc* twice, k1
Rows 2-4: knit
Row 5: *inc, k26, inc* twice, k1
Rows 6-8: knit
Row 9: *inc, k28, inc* twice, k1
Row 10: knit

Work picot edge as folls:-
Row 1: knit

Row 2: purl
Row 3: k1, *yrn, k2tog* to end
Row 4: purl
Rows 5-6: as rows 1-2
Row 7: fold work at row of holes and
knit together, 1st from needle and 1st
from FIRST row of picot, all across row.
Rows 8-20: knit

Shape foot as folls:-
Row 1: k36, k2tog, turn
Row 2: k8, s1, k1, psso, turn
Row 3: using yellow, k8, k2tog, turn
Row 4: using yellow, k8, s1, k1,
psso, turn
Rows 5-6: using red, as rows 3-4
Rows 7-8: using M, as rows 3-4
Rows 9-20: as rows 3-8 twice
Rows 21-24: as rows 3-6. Break off
red and yellow.

Rows 25-28: using M, knit across
all sts
Change to k1, p1 rib to work top
as folls:-
Rows 1-8: M
Rows 9: knit in red
Rows 10-28: still in red, work in rib
Row 29: purl in M
Cast off in M.
Make second bootee to match.

MAKING UP
Join seam using a flat seam. Turn
over top.

Diagonal denim throw

SIZE
Approx 107cms (42ins) squared when shrunk

MATERIALS
Rowan Denim 50g Balls
25 balls Nashville 225
1 pair 4mm (US 6) needles
One 4mm (US 6) circular needle

TENSION
20sts to 28rows = 10cms (4ins) squared over stocking stitch, using 4mm (US 6) needles.

ABBREVIATIONS
See page 79

METHOD
STRIP A (make 3)
Cast on 43sts using 4mm (US 6) needles and work as folls:-
Row 1: k3, *p1, k1, p1, k5* to end
Row 2: k1, *p5, k1, p1, k1* to last 2sts, p2
Row 3: k1, *p1, k1, p1, k5* to last 2sts, p1, k1
Row 4: *k1, p1, k1, p5* to last 3sts, k1, p1, k1
Row 5: k1, p1, *k5, p1, k1, p1* to last st, k1
Row 6: p2, *k1, p1, k1, p5* to last st, k1
Row 7: *k5, p1, k1, p1* to last 3sts, k3
Row 8: p4, *k1, p1, k1, p5* ending last repeat, p4
These 8 rows form patt repeat.
Cont in patt until work measures 20.5cms (10½ins).
Note number of rows worked.
Change to moss stitch and cont until work measures 53cms (21ins). Note number of rows worked.
Repeat work, i.e. noted number of rows of patt, then noted number of rows of moss stitch. Work patt section again. Cast off.

STRIP B (make 2)
Cast on 43sts using 4mm (US 6) needles and work as folls:-
Work in moss stitch for noted number of rows as in strip A.
Change to patt as folls:-
Row 1: *k5, p1, k1, p1* to last 3sts, k3
Row 2: p2, *k1, p1, k1, p5* to last st, k1
Row 3: k1, p1, *k5, p1, k1, p1* to last st, k1
Row 4: *k1, p1, k1, p5* to last 3sts, k1, p1, k1
Row 5: k1, *p1, k1, p1, k5* to last 2sts, p1, k1
Row 6: k1, *p5, k1, p1, k1* to last 2sts, p2
Row 7: k3, *p1, k1, p1, k5* to end
Row 8: p4, *k1, p1, k1, p5* ending last repeat, p4
These 8 rows form patt repeat. Cont in patt for noted number of patt rows in strip A.
Repeat moss stitch and patt sections again and then another moss stitch section. Cast off.

BORDER
Using 4mm (US 6) circular needle cast on 229sts and work 9 rows in moss stitch.
Row 10: moss 7, cast off 215sts, moss 7
On each 7sts (side borders) work in moss until length is same as strips i.e. 5 times the noted number of rows in the moss stitch section.
Next row: moss 7, cast on 215sts, moss 7
NOTE: Make sure the border is not twisted.
Work 9 rows in moss stitch. Cast off in moss stitch.

MAKING UP
Using a flat seam, sew strips together, ensuring that all cast-on edges are at one end and all cast-off edges at the other. Sew A strips and B strips alternately, starting with A.
Pin border into place ensuring cast-off inner edge is sewn to cast-on edge of strips, side borders are sewn to strip length and inner cast-on edge is sewn to strip cast-off edges. Use flat seaming.
Machine wash throw separately in 60° C hot wash with soap powder and tumble dry to shrink. Denim will fade as jeans do with every wash but most colour will come out in this initial wash.

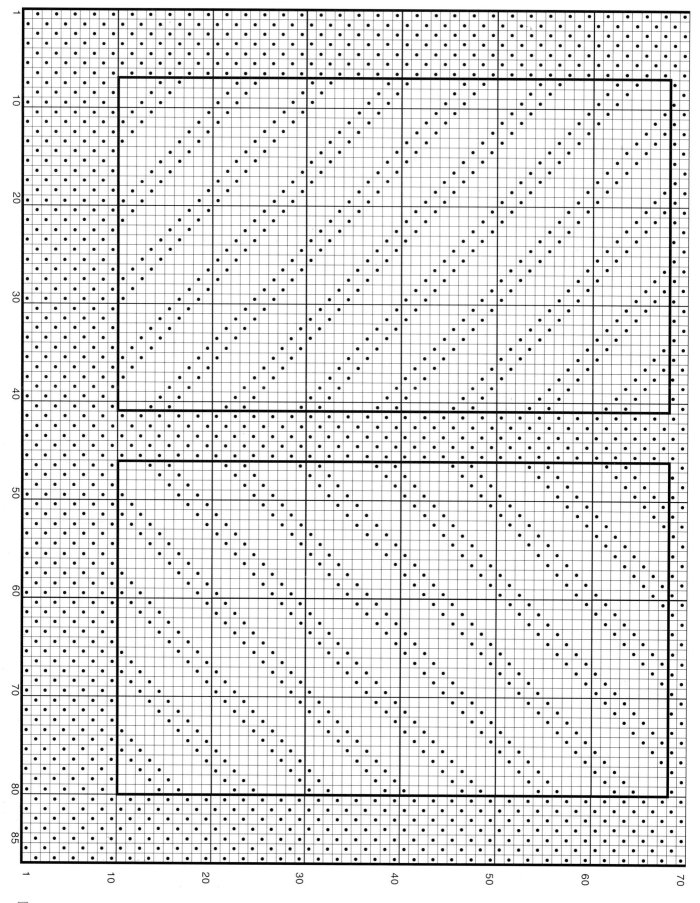

□ P on right side, K on wrong side
□ K on right side, P on wrong side

Diagonal denim cushion
(see page 27)

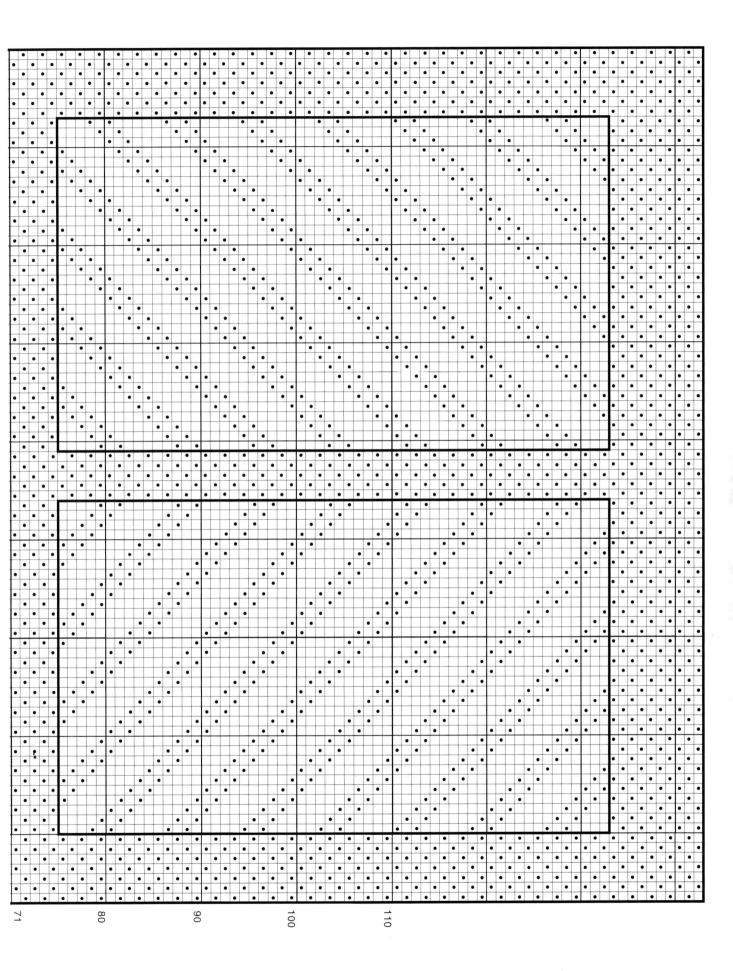

71

80

90

100

110

Diagonal denim cushion

SIZE
43cms (17ins) squared when shrunk

MATERIALS
Rowan Denim 50g Balls
7 balls Nashville 225
1 pair 4mm (US 6) needles
3 buttons of your choice
One 43cm (17in) square feather cushion pad

TENSION
20sts to 28rows = 10cms (4ins) squared over stocking stitch, using 4mm (US 6) needles.

ABBREVIATIONS
See page 79
DIAGRAM
See page 67

METHOD
Front: Using 4mm (US 6) needles cast on 87sts. Work from graph. Cast off.

Back: Cast on 87sts and work in stocking st until work measures 26cms (10¼ins).
Change to moss stitch and work 3 rows in moss stitch.
Row 4: *moss 21, cast off 1st*
3 times, moss 21
Row 5: *moss 21, yrn* 3 times, moss 21
Rows 6-8: moss stitch
Cast off in moss stitch.
Make second piece to match, omitting buttonholes.

MAKING UP
Place cushion right sides together overlapping back cushion pieces.

Making sure buttonhole piece is underneath plain piece, stitch around all 4 sides of cushion. Turn right side out. Machine wash cushion cover separately in 60° C wash with soap powder; tumble dry to shrink. Denim fades with every wash but most colour will come out in initial wash. Sew on buttons. Insert cushion pad.

Knot hat

SIZES
to fit age 1-2 years (2-4 years, 5-6 years)

MATERIALS
Rowan Lightweight DK Wool 25g Skeins
2 skeins Red (M)
1 skein Navy (C)
We used Turquoise 125 (M), and Yellow 13 (C) with small amounts of Black and White for the dog hat; and Navy 108 (M), Red 44 (C) and a small amount of Green 90 for the heart hat
1 pair 3¼mm (US 3) needles and 1 pair 3¾mm (US 5) needles

TENSION
24sts to 32rows = 10cms (4ins) square using 3¾mm (US 5) needles over stocking stitch.

ABBREVIATIONS
See page 79

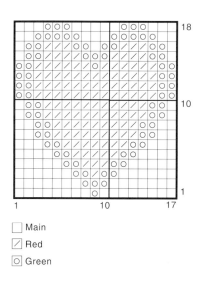

18

10

1

1   10   17

☐ Main
╱ Red
◯ Green

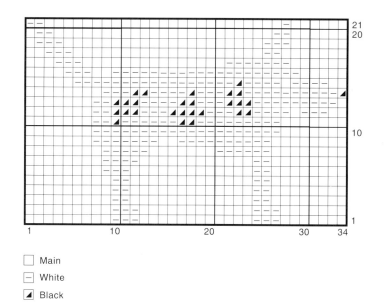

21
20

10

1

1   10   20   30   34

☐ Main
— White
◢ Black

METHOD

Using 3¼mm (US 5) needles and C, cast on 131(139:147)sts. Change to main colour and work as folls:-

Row 1: *k1, p1* to last st, k1

Row 2: Rib 25(27:29), *s1, k2tog, psso, p1, s1, k2tog, psso* rib 67(71:75), * * again, rib 25(27:29)

Row 3: rib 23(25:27), *p3tog, k1, p3tog* rib 63(67:71), * * again; rib 23 (25:27)

Row 4: rib

Row 5: rib 21(23:25), *p3tog, k1, p3tog* rib 59(63:67), * * again, rib 21(23:25)

Row 6: rib 19(21:23), *s1, k2tog, psso, p1, s1, k2tog, psso* rib 55(59:63), * *again rib 19(21:23)

Row 7: rib 17(19:21), *p3tog, k1, p3tog* rib 51(55:59), * *again, rib 17(19:21)   (91:99:107sts)

Row 8: rib 20(22:24), yb, s1, yf, turn: *s1, rib 3, yb, s1, yf, turn: s1, rib 5, yb, s1, yf, turn, s1, rib 7, yb, s1, yf, turn: s1, rib 10, yb, s1, yf, turn, s1, rib 13, yb, s1, yf, turn: s1, rib 16, yb, s1, yf, turn, s1, rib 19, yb, s1, yf, turn: s1, rib 23, yb, s1, yf, turn, s1, rib 27, yb, s1, yf, turn:

SIZES 2 and 3: s1, rib 31, yb, s1, yf, turn, s1, rib 35, yb, s1, yf, turn:*

ALL SIZES: s1, rib 69(77:81), yb, s1, yf, turn, work from * to * again, then s1, rib to end.

Change to 3¾mm (US 5) needles and stocking stitch. Work 2(4:6) rows for dog hat and 6(8:10) rows for heart hat. Place motif as folls:-

DOG: k35(39:43)M, 3 white, 12M, 3 white, 38(42:46)M

HEART: k45(49:53)M, 1 green, 45(49:53)M

Complete motif from chart and then work a further 2(4:6) rows, dec end of last row on SIZE 1 only.

Start shaping as folls:-

Row 1: SIZE 3 only: *k10, k2tog* 8 times, k11

Rows 2-4: stocking stitch

Row 5: SIZES 2 and 3 only: *k9, k2tog* 9 times

Rows 6-8: stocking stitch

Row 9: ALL SIZES: *k8, k2tog* 9 times

Rows 10-12: stocking stitch

Row 13: *k7, k2tog* 9 times

Rows 14-16: stocking stitch

Row 17: *k6, k2tog* 9 times

Row 18: purl

Row 19: *k5, k2tog* 9 times

Row 20: purl

Rows 21-26: Cont dec as set on alt rows   (27sts)

Work 32(36:40) rows without shaping. Change to C and work 14 rows.

Next row: k1, *k2tog* to end

MAKING UP

Run thread through rem sts, pull together and fasten securely. Sew back seam. Weave in any loose ends. Make knot at top of hat pulling contrast end through (see photograph on pages 28-29).

Knot hat   **65**

(see page 28-29)

Hearts and stars baby blanket

SIZE
59cms (23ins) by 72cm (28ins), excluding edging

MATERIALS
Rowan Cotton Glace 50g Balls

6 balls Delft 782 (A)

5 balls Sky 749 (B)

2 balls Matador 742

1 ball of the foll colours:- Kiwi 443, Parade 430, Bubblegum 441, Terracotta 786 and Banana 444

1 pair 3¾mm (US 5) needles

TENSION
23sts to 32rows = 10cms (4ins) squared over stocking stitch, using 3¾mm (US 5) needles.

ABBREVIATIONS
See page 79

METHOD
Using 3¾mm (US 5) needles and B, cast on 138sts. Work 4 rows in moss stitch. Please use the intarsia method of colour knitting.

Row 5: *moss 3B, k24A* 5 times, moss 3B

Row 6: *moss 3B, p24A* 5 times, moss 3B

Rows 7-8: as rows 5-6

Row 9: Start heart motifs: work motifs in random colours using graphs A, B, A, B, A, across work; *moss 3B, k11A, 1 for heart, 12A* 5 times, moss 3B

Rows 10-32: complete heart motifs

Rows 33-36: as rows 5-8

Row 37: using B *moss 3, k24* 5 times, moss 3B

Rows 38-40: moss stitch

Rows 41-43: as rows 5-7

Row 44: Start star motifs, work motifs in random colours using graphs C, D, C, D, C across work; *moss 3B, p3A, 1 for star, 15A, 2 for star, 3A* 5 times, moss 3B

Rows 45-69: complete star motifs

Rows 70-72: as rows 6-8

Rows 73-76: as rows 37-40

Rows 5-76 form patt repeat.

Repeat these twice more, then rows 5-40 again.

Cast off in moss st.

EDGING (make 52)
Using 3¾mm (US 5) needles and B, cast on 13sts. Work 2 rows moss stitch. Cont in moss stitch dec each end of next and foll alt rows to 3sts. Work 1 row. K3tog, fasten off.

MAKING UP
Weave in any loose ends. Sew triangles around edge of blanket, 11 on short sides and 15 on long sides.

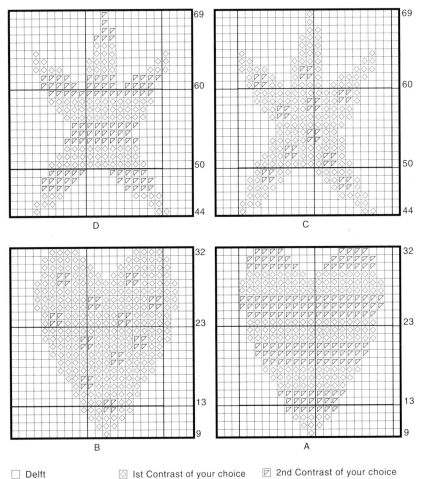

□ Delft   ◪ lst Contrast of your choice   ◩ 2nd Contrast of your choice

Hearts and stars cushion

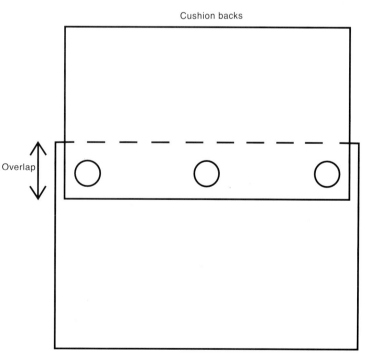

SIZE
31cms (12ins) squared

MATERIALS
Rowan Cotton Glace 50g Balls

2 balls Delft 782 (A)

3 balls Sky 749 (B)

1 ball of the foll colours:- Kiwi 443, Parade 430, Bubblegum 441, Terracotta 786,

Matador 724 and Banana 444

1 pair 3¾mm (US 5) needles

3 buttons of your choice

One 31cm (12in) square feather cushion pad

TENSION
23sts to 32rows = 10cms (4ins) squared over stocking stitch, using 3¾mm (US 5) needles.

ABBREVIATIONS
See page 79

METHOD
Front: Using 3¾mm (US 5) needles and B, cast on 54sts and work 4 rows in moss stitch. Please use the intarsia method of colour knitting.

Rows 5-76: follow instructions for blanket NOTING graph repeats are A, B, A and C, D, C and * * instructions are 3 times.

Work rows 5-40 again. Cast off in moss stitch.

Back: Using 3¾mm (US 5) needles and B cast on 54sts and work 56 rows in stocking stitch. Change to moss stitch and work 3 rows.

Row 4: * moss 11, cast off 3sts*
3 times, moss 12

Row 5: moss 12, *cast on 3sts, moss 11* 3 times

Rows 6-8: moss stitch

Cast off in moss stitch using A.

Make second piece to match, omitting buttonholes.

EDGING (make 28)
Using 3¾mm (US 5) needles and B, cast on 13sts. Work 2 rows moss

stitch. Cont in moss stitch dec each end of next and foll alt rows to 3sts. Work 1 row. K3tog, fasten off.

MAKING UP
Weave in any loose ends. Pin or tack edging (7 per side) to cushion fronts with points to centre. Place cushion backs to cushion front, right sides together, ensuring that when overlapping the buttonhole edge is underneath the button edge. Sew around cushion, through all thicknesses, trapping edging in place as you stitch. Turn rightside out. Sew on buttons. Insert cushion pad.

Cushions General Diagram

Cushion backs

Overlap

Symbol	Color
+ 219 Gooseberry	↖ 215 Rosso	− 263 Bleached	↗ 254 Flame
(M) 221 Basil	／ 217 Powder	◢ 252 Black	◇ 229 Popcorn
			• 240 Raspberry

Bunny shopping bag

(see page 32)

Bunny shopping bag

SIZE
25cms (10ins) wide
31cms (12ins) deep
Side and base panel depth 3cms (1¼ins)

MATERIALS
Rowan Handknit DK Cotton 50g Balls
2 balls Basil 221
1 ball Bleached 263
1 ball Gooseberry 219
Small amounts of Raspberry 240, Rosso 215, Popcorn 229, Flame 254, Black 252 and Powder 217
1 pair 4mm (US 6) needles and 1 pair 3¾mm (US 5) needles

TENSION
20sts to 28rows = 10cms (4ins) squared over stocking stitch, using 4mm (US 6) needles.

ABBREVIATIONS
See page 79

METHOD AND MAKING UP
Using 3¾mm (US 5) needles and Gooseberry 219 cast on 40sts. Work 10 rows in moss stitch. Change to 4mm (US 6) needles and M and stocking stitch. Work rows 1-80 from graph. Please use intarsia method for all colour work.
Row 81: Change to 3¾mm (US 5) needles and Gooseberry 219, and knit.
Rows 82-90: work in moss stitch. Cast off in moss stitch.
Make second piece to match.
These two pieces make the front and back of the shopping bag.
To make the side and base panel, cast on 7sts using Gooseberry 219 and 3¾mm (US 5) needles. Work in moss st until band fits around both sides and base of bag.
Pin pieces together inside out and stitch together.

HANDLES (make 2)
Cast on 7sts using Basil 221 and 3¾mm (US 5) needles. Work in moss st until handle measures 30cms (12ins). Pin handles to bag on right side and stitch into place, one on each side (see photo on page 32).

Rooster shoe bag

SIZE
30cms (12ins) wide by 36cms (14¼ins) deep

MATERIALS
Rowan Handknit DK Cotton 50g Balls
3 balls Powder 217 (M)
Small amounts of Rosso 215, Flame 254, Bleached 263, Turkish plum 277, Popcorn 229 and Basil 221
1 pair 4mm (US 6) needles and 1 pair 3¼mm (US 3) needles

TENSION
20sts to 28rows = 10cms (4ins) squared over stocking stitch, using 4mm (US 6) needles

Bunny shopping bag and Rooster shoe bag

(see pages 32 and 33)

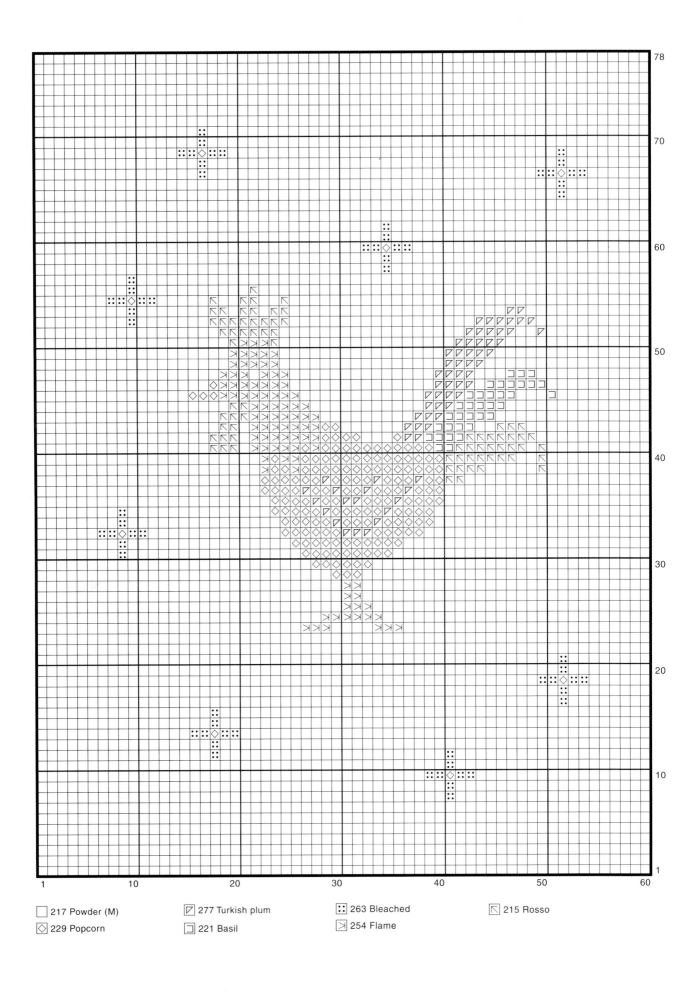

☐ 217 Powder (M)	☑ 277 Turkish plum	∷ 263 Bleached	◱ 215 Rosso
◇ 229 Popcorn	◲ 221 Basil	⊠ 254 Flame	

Rooster shoe bag

(see page 33)

METHOD

Using 4mm (US 6) needles and M cast on 60sts. Work in stocking stitch and using the intarsia method for picture knitting, follow graph rows 1-78.
Row 79: Change to 3¼mm (US 3) needles, *k3, p3* to end

Rows 80-94: as row 79
Row 95: *k3, p3, k1, yrn, k2tog, p3* to end
Rows 96-100: as row 79
Change to Turkish plum 277 and cast off in rib.
Make second piece to match.

CORD

Take 6 long strands of M and knot at one end. Then make plait using 2 ends of yarn per strand. Plait until cord measures about 80cms (31½ins). Tie knot in end.

MAKING UP

Weave in any loose ends. Right sides facing, stitch together bag sides and base. Thread cord through eyelet holes, and tie both ends together with one tight knot. Snip off original knots to neaten.

Wee Willy Winkie hat

SIZES

To fit age 0-9 months (1-2 years, 3-4 years, 5-6 years)

MATERIALS

Rowan Designer DK Wool 50g Balls
1 ball of White 649 for all sizes
1 ball of M for sizes 0-9 months and 1-2 years, and 2 balls for all other sizes
For M we used Red 634 /Green 68 (see photograph)
1 pair 4mm (US 6) needles and 1 pair 3¼mm (US 3) needles

TENSION

24sts to 32rows = 10cms (4ins) square using 4mm (US 6) needles over stocking stitch.

ABBREVIATIONS

See page 79

METHOD

Using 3¼mm (US 3) needles and M cast on 88(96:108:116)sts and work 10(12:14:16) rows in k1, p1 rib. Change to 4mm (US 6) needles, stocking stitch and stripe pattern of 2 rows white, 2 rows M.

Work 16(18:20:22) rows.
Start shaping:-
Next row: *k20(22:25:27) s1, k1, psso, k2tog, k20(22:25:27)* twice
Work 3 rows without shaping.
Next row: *k19(21:24:26) s1, k1, psso, k2tog, k19(21:24:26)* twice
Work 3 rows without shaping.
Next row: *k18(20:23:25) s1, k1, psso, k2tog, k18(20:23:25)* twice
Cont as set, dec on every foll 4th row to 32sts.
Dec as set on every alt row to 12sts.
Run thread through remaining sts, pull tight and secure.

MAKING UP

Stitch up centre back seam. Weave in any loose ends. Make pom-pom using M and attach securely to top of hat.

stripy cushion

SIZE
36cms (14ins) squared

MATERIALS
Rowan Handknit DK Cotton 50g Balls
3 balls Rosso 215 (M)
1 ball each of Powder 217, Basil 221, Flame 254 and Sunkissed 231
1 pair 4mm (US 6) needles and 1 pair 3¼mm (US 3) needles
4 buttons of your choice
One 36cm (14in) square feather cushion pad

TENSION
20sts to 28rows = 10cms (4ins) squared over stocking stitch, using 4mm (US 6) needles.

ABBREVIATIONS
See page 79

DIAGRAM
See page 67

METHOD
Front: Using 4mm (US 6) needles and Rosso 215 cast on 70sts. Work in stocking stitch in the foll sequence:-
Rows 1-7: Rosso 215
Rows 8-11: Flame 254
Rows 12-18: Sunkissed 231
Rows 19-21: Powder 217
Rows 22-25: Basil 221
Rows 26-28: Flame 254
Rows 29-31: Rosso 215
Rows 32-34: Flame 254
Rows 35-38: Sunkissed 231
Rows 39-46: Basil 221
Rows 47-51: Powder 217
Rows 52-54: Rosso 215
Rows 55-61: Flame 254
Rows 62-65: Rosso 215
Rows 66-68: Basil 221
Rows 69-76: Sunkissed 231

Rows 77-80: Powder 217
Rows 81-84: Rosso 215
Rows 85-88: Flame 254
Rows 89-93: Basil 221
Rows 94-98: Sunkissed 231
Rows 98-99: Rosso 215
Cast off in Rosso 215.

Back: Using 4mm (US 6) needles and M, cast on 70sts and work 50 rows in stocking stitch. Change to 3¼mm (US 3) needles and work 2 rows k2, p2 rib.
Row 3: rib 10, cast off 1st, *rib 15, cast off 1st* 3 times, rib 11
Row 4: rib 11, yrn, *rib 15, yrn* 3 times, rib 10
Work 2 more rows in rib and cast off in contrast colour of your choice.
Make second piece to match, omitting buttonholes.

POINTED EDGING
Using 4mm (US 6) needles and all colours randomly, but in complete pattern repeats, cast on 2sts.
Row 1: k2
Row 2: inc, k1
Row 3: k1, p1, inc
Row 4: inc, k1, p1, k1
Rows 5-8: moss stitch, inc at shaped edge on every row   (9sts)
Row 9: moss stitch
Rows 10-16: Dec at shaped edge on each row, moss stitch   (2sts)
Repeat rows 1-16 until straight edge fits around edge of cushion.

MAKING UP
Pin edging around edge of front cushion with points towards the centre. Place right sides together, making sure the buttonhole back piece is under the button piece. The back pieces will overlap to make a 36cm (14in) square to match the front.
Stitch around all 4 sides of cushion inside out, making sure you trap edging between the front and back pieces. Turn right side out and sew on buttons of your choice. Insert cushion pad.

star rucksack

SIZE
38cms (15ins) long by 28cms (11ins) wide by 8cms (3ins) deep

MATERIALS
Rowan Handknit DK Cotton 50g Balls
5 balls Powder 217
2 balls Popcorn 229
1 ball of foll colours:- Basil 221, Gooseberry 219, Summer pudding 243, Flame 254 and Gerba 223
1 pair 4mm (US 6) needles, 1 pair 3¾mm (US 5) needles and a stitch holder
½ metre (20in) of lining fabric of your choice
1 button of your choice

TENSION
20sts to 28rows = 10cms (4ins) squared over stocking stitch, using 4mm (US 6) needles.

ABBREVIATIONS
See page 79

POCKET
Using 4mm (US 6) needles and M cast on 25sts and work 40 rows in stocking stitch. Leave on holder.

METHOD
PART A: FLAP
Using 4mm (US 6) needles and M cast on 49sts and work as follows:-
Row 1: *k1, p1* to last st, k1
Row 2: *k1, p1* 14 times, turn
Row 3: sp, moss 10, turn
Row 4: sp, moss 14, turn
Row 5: sp, moss 18, turn
Row 6: sp, moss 10, cast off 1st, moss 11, turn
Row 7: sp, moss 10, yrn, moss 14, turn
Row 8: sk, moss 28, turn
Row 9: sk, moss 31, turn
Row 10: sp, moss 34, turn
Row 11: sp, moss 36, turn
Row 12: sp, moss 38, turn
Row 13: sp, moss 40, turn
Row 14: sp, moss 42, turn
Row 15: sp, moss 44, turn
Row 16: sp, moss 46, turn
Row 17: sp, moss 47, turn
Row 18: moss 49
Rows 19-36: moss

Star Rucksack
No lining on flap

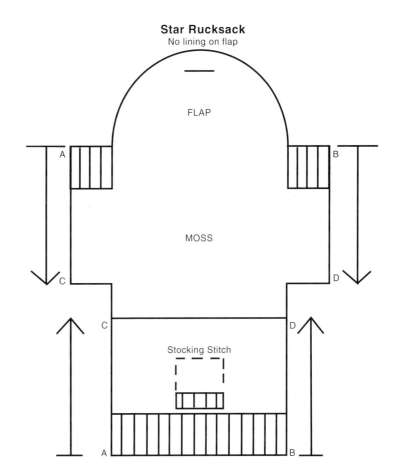

Sew C to C & D to D making corners.
Then put A to A, B to B
Sewing down side of rucksack,
A to C and B to D

(see page 37)

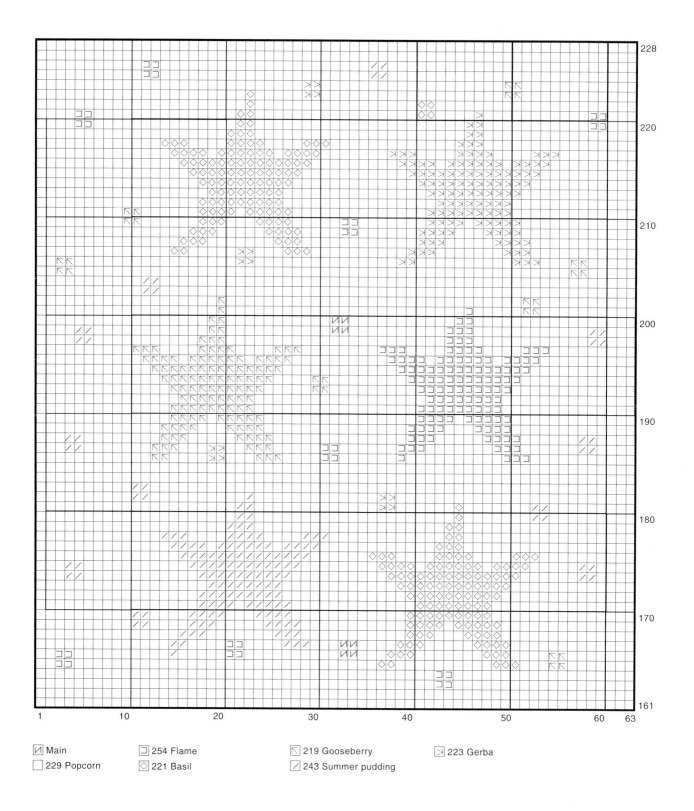

228
220
210
200
190
180
170
161

1   10   20   30   40   50   60 63

| ⊠ Main | ⊐ 254 Flame | ⊡ 219 Gooseberry | ⊠ 223 Gerba |
| ☐ 229 Popcorn | ◇ 221 Basil | ⟋ 243 Summer pudding | |

PART B: BACK

Row 37: cast on 21sts, *p3, k3*
twice, p3, moss 55
Row 38: cast on 21sts, *k3 p3* twice,
k3, moss 61, *k3, p3* twice, k3
Row 39: *p3, k3* twice, p3, moss 61,
p3, k3 twice, p3
Row 40: *k3, p3* twice, k3, moss 61,
k3, p3 twice, k3
Row 41: as row 39
Row 42: *k3, p1, cast off 1st, p1*
twice, k3, moss 61, * k3, p1, cast off
1st, p1* twice, k3
Row 43: *p3, k1, yrn, k1* twice, p3,
moss 61, *p3, k1, yrn, k1* twice, p3
Row 44: as row 40
Row 45-62: as rows 39-40
Row 63-140: moss stitch

PART C: BASE

Rows 141-2: cast off 14sts, moss
to end   (63sts)
Rows 143-160: moss stitch

PART D: FRONT

Rows 161-228: follow graph, placing
pocket on row 212: pattern 19, place
next 25sts on holder, pattern across
25sts of pocket, pattern to end
Row 229: Change to M, knit
Row 230: purl

Row 231: *k3, p3* 10 times, k3
Row 232: *p3, k3* 10 times, p3
Row 233-248: as 231-232
Row 249: as 231
Row 250: *k1, yrn, k1, p3* 10 times,
k1, yrn, k1
Row 252: as 232
Rows 253-256: as 231-232
Cast off.

STRAPS (make 2)

Using 3¾mm (US 5) needles and M
cast on 7sts. Work in moss stitch
until strap measures 46cms (18ins).
Cast off.

POCKET TOP

Using 3¾mm (US 5) needles and M,
right side facing, knit across pocket
sts, cast on 1st.
Work 5 rows in *k2, p2* rib. Cast off
in rib.
Slip stitch pocket and pocket top
into place.

MAKING UP

Make a lining template by drawing
around the flat knitted bag shape on
to lining fabric, omitting the flap and
adding a 1cm (½in) seam allowance all
found. Cut out lining shape. Look at
diagram. Sew up bag and lining, and
place together (all seams facing each
other). Cut off lining where rib is
shown, so lining will fit into bag
with top rib having no lining. Pin
lining to top inside edge, turn under
and machine into place.
Make two 30cm (12in) plaited ties
using 6 strands of yarn (2 strands
in each plait piece). Sew these
into sides of back lining and
thread the ties through eyelet
holes in the rib at top.
To line straps of bag, cut two 56cm
(22in) lengths of fabric – this will
allow for the pull when sewing the
lining to the 46cm (18in) straps of
knitting. Cut the lining fabric 1cm (½in)
larger than the width of the strap,
all the way round. Fold in raw
edges as you sew down the lining.
Make sure both straps are the
same length.
When machining together the straps,
make sure the bobbin thread of your
sewing machine has the strap colour
and the top thread has the lining colour.
Finish off by sewing on the straps and
adding a button in the centre front of
your bag above the pocket. Trim off
all loose threads.

Tractor rucksack

SIZE
28cms (11ins) wide by 38cm (15ins) deep

MATERIALS
Rowan Handknit DK Cotton 50g Balls
3 balls Sailor Blue 232 (M)
1 ball Gooseberry 219
Small amounts of Popcorn 229, Rosso 215 and Bleached 263
1 pair 4mm (US 6) needles

TENSION
20sts to 28rows = 10cms (4ins)
squared over stocking stitch, using
4mm (US 6) needles.

ABBREVIATIONS
See page 79

METHOD
Using 4mm (US 6) needles and
Gooseberry 219, cast on 55sts and
work 12 rows in stocking stitch.
Row 13: k25, cast off 1st, k3, cast off
1st, k25
Row 14: p25, yrn, p3, yrn, p25
Rows 15-18: stocking stitch
Change to M and work 120 rows in
stocking stitch.
Row 121: Place tractor from chart,
k20 M, 3 Gooseberry 219, 32 M
Rows 122-156: work tractor
Rows 157-188: stocking stitch
Change to Gooseberry 219 and work
18 rows in stocking stitch. Cast off.

CORD
Using 4mm (US 6) needles and
Gooseberry 219, cast on 6sts and
work in stocking stitch for 150cms
(59ins). Cast off.

MAKING UP
Weave in any loose ends. Fold bag in
half, right sides together, and stitch
side seams. Fold green top in half and
slip stitch into place, all seams to the
inside of the bag.
Thread cord through holes at top.
Stitch ends to side seams at bottom
corners of bag, making sure that
cord from left-hand hole is sewn to
right-hand corner, and cord
from right-hand hole is sewn to
left-hand corner.

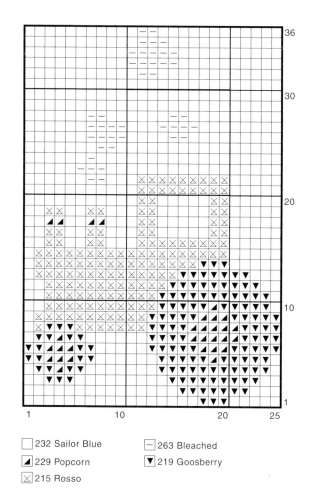

☐ 232 Sailor Blue   ⊟ 263 Bleached

◢ 229 Popcorn   ▼ 219 Goosberry

☒ 215 Rosso

Reindeer scarf and hat

scarf

SIZE

20cms (8ins) wide by 107cms (42ins) long. One size.

MATERIALS

Rowan Designer DK Wool 50g Balls
1 ball of White 649
1 ball of Brick red 632
1 pair 4mm (US 6) needles and 1 pair 3¼mm (US 3) needles

TENSION

24sts and 32rows = 10cms (4ins) square using 4mm (US 6)
needles over stocking stitch.

ABBREVIATIONS

See page 79

| | Scarf and Size 1 Hat |
| Size 2 Hat |
| Size 3 Hat |

◻ (with diagonal) 632 Brick Red
◻ 649 White

Size 1
Size 2
Size 3

(see page 39)

METHOD

Using 3¼mm (US 3) needles and Brick red 632, cast on 49sts and work 10 rows in moss stitch.

Change to 4mm (US 6) needles and stocking stitch, with a k2 beginning and end of every purl row, work rows 1-46 from graph.

Change to stripe patt of 2 rows Brick red 632, 2 rows white 649 and keeping k2 edging cont until work measures approx 74cms (29ins), ending with a red stripe. Turn graph upside down and work rows 46-1.

Change to Brick red 632 and knit 1 row. Change to 3¼mm (US 3) needles and work 10 rows in moss stitch. Cast off in moss stitch.

MAKING UP

Weave in any loose ends and press using a damp cloth over work.

Hat

SIZES

To fit age 1-2 years (2-4 years, 5-6 years)

MATERIALS

Rowan Designer DK Wool 50g Balls
1 ball of White 649
1 ball of 632 Brick red
1 pair 4mm (US 6) needles and 1 pair 3¼mm (US 3) needles

TENSION

24sts to 32rows = 10cms (4ins) square using 4mm (US 6) needles over stocking stitch.

ABBREVIATIONS

See page 79

METHOD

Using 3¼mm (US 3) needles and Brick red 632 cast on 43(47:51)sts and work 25 rows in moss stitch.
Row 26: moss 1(3:5) *inc, moss 7* 5 times, inc, moss 1(3:5)   53:57)sts

Change to 4mm (US 6) needles and stocking stitch.
Work from graph rows 11-36 for first size and 1-36 for other sizes.
All sizes: Using Brick red 632:
k3, cast off 43(47:51)sts, k3. Leave on spare needle.
Make second piece to match.

TIES (make 2)

Join side seams of hat. On 6sts and using 4mm (US 6) needles and stocking stitch, work in 2-row stripes of each colour until tie measures 20(23:26)cms, 8(9:10)ins long.
Cast off.
Work other tie to match.

MAKING UP

Turn hat inside out, making sure ties are not caught. Stitch top seam of hat. Weave in any loose ends. Turn hat right side out. Tie ties to fit child's head.